American Catholic Higher Education in the 21st Century: Critical Challenges

Edited by Robert R. Newton

CONTRIBUTORS:

J.A. Appleyard, S.J.

Jessica A. Greene

James L. Heft, S.M.

Michael J. Himes

Robert J. Kaslyn, S.J.

William P. Leahy, S.J.

David J. O'Brien

LINDEN LANE PRESS AT BOSTON COLLEGE

CHESTNUT HILL, MASSACHUSETTS

A report from the Boston College Sesquicentennial Symposium on Catholic Higher Education at Boston College in October 2013

Linden Lane Press at Boston College
140 Commonwealth Avenue
3 Lake Street Building
Chestnut Hill, Massachusetts 02467
617–552–4820
www.bc.edu/lindenlanepress

ISBN 978-0-9816416-6-9
Library of Congress Control Number: 2014958093

Printed in the USA

Contents

vii **INTRODUCTION**
Critical Challenges
WILLIAM P. LEAHY, S.J., PRESIDENT, BOSTON COLLEGE

1 The History of American Catholic Higher Education
DAVID J. O'BRIEN, LOYOLA PROFESSOR EMERITUS, COLLEGE OF THE HOLY CROSS

17 The Catholic Intellectual Tradition and Integral Humanism
MICHAEL J. HIMES, PROFESSOR, THEOLOGY DEPARTMENT, BOSTON COLLEGE

33 Student Formation in Catholic Colleges and Universities
J.A. APPLEYARD, S.J., PROFESSOR EMERITUS, BOSTON COLLEGE

61 "Catholic" as Descriptive of a University: A Canonical Perspective
ROBERT J. KASLYN, S.J., DEAN OF THE SCHOOL OF CANON LAW,
THE CATHOLIC UNIVERSITY OF AMERICA

89 Leadership in Catholic Higher Education
JAMES L. HEFT, S.M., ALTON M. BROOKS PROFESSOR OF RELIGION,
UNIVERSITY OF SOUTHERN CALIFORNIA

117 Looking Forward: Catholic Higher Education in the 21st Century
WILLIAM P. LEAHY, S.J., PRESIDENT, BOSTON COLLEGE

124 **APPENDIX A**
Survey of Catholic College Presidents
JESSICA A. GREENE, DIRECTOR, OFFICE OF INSTITUTIONAL RESEARCH,
BOSTON COLLEGE

144 **APPENDIX B**
Participants in the Boston College Sesquicentennial Symposium
on Catholic Higher Education

146 **CONTRIBUTORS**

Critical Challenges

WILLIAM P. LEAHY, S.J.
PRESIDENT, BOSTON COLLEGE

As part of its Sesquicentennial celebration, Boston College invited leading Catholic educators to a symposium concerning the future of Catholic higher education in the United States. Participants gathered from October 22–24, 2013, at BC's Connors Family Retreat and Conference Center in Dover, Massachusetts. They discussed four critical issues requiring engagement by Catholic educational leaders: (1) strengthening awareness of and commitment to the Catholic intellectual tradition on Catholic campuses; (2) ensuring the personal and religious formation of students; (3) clarifying the relationship of Catholic colleges and universities to the Church, and (4) identifying and preparing future leaders of Catholic postsecondary institutions. The essays in this volume provided context for the days at Dover, and are intended to spotlight and urge action on critical challenges facing American Catholic higher education today.

The symposium's focus reflects the profound changes in Catholic life and education during the last 50 years. In 1960, the Catholic community in the United States had few concerns about the future of the Catholic intellectual tradition, effectiveness of Catholic colleges and universities in moral and faith development of students, connections with the Church, and recruitment of presidents and other academic leaders. Catholics were growing in number, confidence, and acceptance by mainstream culture, and they particularly rejoiced in John Kennedy's election as the first Catholic president of the United States. Similarly, Catholic higher education had been advancing steadily in scope, enrollment, quality, and complexity during the first half of the 20th century, particularly in undergraduate programs. Catholic colleges and universities increased from 63 in 1900, enrolling 4,200 students, to more than 230 educating approximately 300,000 in 1960. Of 314 institutions on the accredited list issued by the American Council of Education in 1920, only 26 were Catholic schools, about 20 percent of Catholic higher education. By 1960, 87 percent of Catholic institutions of higher learning met the standards of their regional accrediting associations.

Neo-scholastic philosophy dominated the curriculum of Catholic colleges and universities, which had a clear and compelling sense of purpose: to protect the faith of Catholics and to make it possible for more members of the Church to obtain undergraduate, graduate, and professional degrees. According to traditional Catholic educational theory, collegiate training should enrich students personally and spiritually, not concentrate solely on intellectual development. Consequently, in addition to academic knowledge, Catholic postsecondary institutions sought to transmit Catholic traditions, values, and principles, hoping to influence their students and the wider society.

These institutions maintained a cordial relationship with the hierarchy and institutional Church, and disputes about policy or doctrine were few and seldom became public. Furthermore, the dioceses and religious orders of men and women that had founded institutions of higher education had numerous candidates for leadership positions, and few even considered selecting lay people to be presidents. In the early 1960s many Catholics felt indebted to Catholic schools, which had enabled many of them to advance professionally, socially, and financially.

But the comfortable, tight-knit Catholic subculture and higher education world began to disintegrate in the 1960s as Catholics and their fellow citizens in the United States confronted a range of social, political, religious, and ideological tensions resulting from growing secularism in modern society as well as from deep differences over civil rights, opposition to the Vietnam War, and reforms proposed by the Second Vatican Council. Gradually, the previous consensus regarding the nature, characteristics, and meaning of Catholic education began to dissolve and the way forward became less clear and more challenging.

Needed was a fresh, compelling vision rooted in the Catholic intellectual and religious heritage and able to respond effectively to new circumstances. But many of the clerics and religious in charge of Catholic higher education before the 1960s lacked the insight, flexibility, and awareness of modern cultural and educational trends necessary to help the Catholic community respond effectively to changing circumstances. Their training and perspective emphasized character formation and an apologetical approach, one relying on long-standing arguments to defend Catholic teachings and belief. Too many Catholic leaders prior to the opening of the Second Vatican Council in 1962 clung to tradition, orthodoxy, and religious discipline as protection against a more secular environment.

However, change began to sweep Catholic higher education in the late 1960s. Seeking to improve their reputation in American academic culture, numerous Catholic colleges and universities in the 1970s began to professionalize and give greater weight to strictly professional criteria in personnel decisions rather than on ensuring that faculty understood and supported Catholic beliefs, values, and traditions. Administrators often offered positions to non-Catholic applicants with degrees from prestigious secular schools rather than Catholics holding doctorates from Catholic institutions or currently employed by Catholic institutions.

Over time, the culture in Catholic schools became less supportive of religious and pastoral goals previously so dominant in Catholic higher education. In the 1970s and 1980s, faculty in Catholic colleges and universities, like their secular counterparts, increasingly questioned the validity and value of long-standing reliance on Thomistic philosophy as the integrating principle and foundation of Catholic education. Many came to conclude that the traditional Catholic ideal of "faith seeking understanding" was outdated and no longer viable in the modern university. Moreover, too seldom were recently hired faculty and administrators provided the opportunity and resources to appreciate the origins, evolution, and Catholic elements and ethos of their institutions.

Furthermore, little attention was given to strengthening awareness of and commitment to the Catholic intellectual tradition on campuses and in Catholic culture. In a sense, the Catholic intellectual tradition is to the Catholic Church as memory is to an individual. Regrettably, most schools after 1970 did not make it a priority to identify, hire, and reward faculty willing and able to teach and write about ideas, values, and approaches shaped by Catholic life and culture. They did not encourage experts to research and write monographs presenting Catholic perspectives on issues and drawn from such influential Catholic thinkers as Augustine, Bonaventure, Thomas Aquinas, and Newman. Nor did the Catholic literary imagination receive appropriate emphasis. The curriculum in most Catholic institutions of higher education did not provide undergraduate and graduate students with sufficient opportunity to learn about the Catholic intellectual tradition. Consequently, few of them developed an appreciation of the intellectual heritage of Catholicism or drew from it, and the vast majority of students were unable to help communicate key Catholic insights and understandings to succeeding generations.

Another major challenge for the Catholic community in the United States in recent decades has been handing on the faith to younger members of the Catholic Church. Until the widespread changes in the late 1960s, Catholic colleges and universities placed a high priority on enabling students to understand and appreciate Catholic traditions, values, and principles. Faculty and administrators in Catholic schools commonly encouraged the subordination of scholarship and academic status to teaching, spiritual concerns, and involvement with students, reflecting their religious convictions and sympathies. Most undergraduates enrolled in Catholic higher education before the 1980s came from Catholic families, and adherence to Catholic faith and practice was presumed.

But conditions have changed dramatically in recent decades. Many faculty members in Catholic higher education today do not share a commitment to the personal and religious formation of students for many reasons. The concept of student formation is not familiar to them, and it lacks a compelling rationale incorporating recent insights regarding young adult development, pastoral theology, and pedagogy. In addition, similar to their secular counterparts, they have a narrower definition of their roles, focusing almost exclusively on what happens in the classroom and their students' academic progress. The topic of student formation can make them uneasy, and large numbers of professors regard it as outside their responsibility and better left to personnel in campus ministry and student affairs. Their own education concentrated on intellectual development with little reference to personal formation, and many believe that students should and will find their own way, just as they did as undergraduates.

In addition, students in Catholic postsecondary institutions today are more diverse and often will declare themselves to be spiritual but not religious. Many, even those from Catholic backgrounds, come to college without strong faith foundations or regard themselves as "unchurched," lacking the knowledge, understanding, and regular practice of the faith. Nevertheless, many students are hungry for role models and serious discussions with peers and older adults about life issues. A 2005 UCLA study by the Higher Education

Research Institute titled *The Spiritual Life of College Students: A National Study of College Students' Search for Meaning and Purpose* reported that 76 percent of students in the national sample were searching for meaning and purpose in life and 47 percent were seeking opportunities to grow spiritually. Meeting those desires has to be a top priority for Catholic colleges and universities.

The third major challenge explored at the BC Sesquicentennial symposium concerned the sometimes confused and neuralgic relationship between Catholic institutions of higher education and the official Church in the last 40 years, particularly with certain bishops and staff in Vatican offices. Many of the issues result from different understandings of episcopal authority, the role of theologians today, and the nature of the contemporary Catholic college or university. For example, some bishops have felt compelled in recent decades to call for restrictions or even termination of theologians at Catholic institutions over orthodoxy concerns. Disagreements have also surfaced when Catholic schools have sponsored speakers or conferred awards, especially honorary degrees, on public figures who support views counter to the Catholic Church. Furthermore, publication of the papal document *Ex Corde Ecclesiae* in 1990 resulted in differing interpretations about the purpose of Catholic colleges and universities and the role of the local bishop in regard to these institutions.

Most Catholics do not understand the intricacies and principles of canon law as it applies to Catholic higher education. Perhaps no issue has been more difficult to grasp than the validity and consequences of the decision by many Catholic colleges and universities starting in the late 1960s to separately incorporate themselves from the founding religious community. Some have argued that such moves to transfer assets to the school's board of trustees may have been legal civilly but not canonically, unless formal approval from the Vatican was obtained, a step that the majority of schools did not take.

Questions remain to this day about how schools that "separately incorporated" relate to the Church as required in current canon law. Attempts to provide answers must proceed carefully to avoid harming the authority and commitment of boards of trustees, so critical for the ongoing viability of institutions, or casting doubt on the validity of financial transactions approved by lay boards, especially issuance of bonds.

Another important canonical issue is how a college or university founded by a religious community maintains its link to the Church when members of the founding group no longer live and work at a particular institution.

Currently, the tie to the Church is through the religious order; and given the decline in the religious congregations of men and women, soon a number of schools will not have canonically recognized communities located on their campuses. Both the Church and Catholic higher education have changed greatly in the last 50 years, and each is now challenged to clarify its relationship to the other. They also must determine how to respond effectively to the reality of declining numbers of religious and the pressing need to sustain their distinctive missions and service to the Catholic community and contemporary society.

Symposium participants also focused on the crucial issue of identifying and preparing future leaders for Catholic higher education. Before the early 1960s, clergy and religious held almost all senior posts in Catholic colleges and universities outside business and professional divisions. For example, in 1960, no lay person served as dean of colleges of liberal arts in the 28 Jesuit schools; in 1988, there were 19 lay deans, and in 2014, only four Jesuit institutions have Jesuit deans. The steady decline in the number of men and women from founding religious orders or dioceses for leadership positions has resulted in the appointment of more lay men and women, and those numbers will increase as current presidents who are priests or men and women religious retire. Finding replacements with the necessary academic and religious qualifications is a growing challenge.

The survey of Catholic college and university presidents in preparation for the BC gathering found 57 percent of presidents responding were lay people; and of them, only about a quarter were the first lay president at their institutions, indicating that the shift from religious to lay is already well established. Such a transition poses significant challenges to the future of Catholic colleges and universities. According to the data, clerics and male/female religious assumed senior leadership roles after a lengthy religious and academic formation, but most lay presidents came to their roles with significantly different backgrounds. Only 56 percent of them reported they were familiar with the mission of their institution when appointed, compared to 80 percent of presidents who were religious. Moreover, only 16 percent of lay presidents reported enrollment in graduate theology programs, in contrast to the 82 percent of presidents who were religious.

Leaders of Catholic institutions of higher education must be able to provide an appropriately Catholic vision and clear decisions for their schools. Critical to that effort is an in-depth knowledge of Catholic theology and

Catholic culture, especially in moments of conflict or when determining strategic directions. But individuals with that background and commitment are not readily available, as recent presidential search committees can attest. Thus, there is widespread agreement about the urgent need to identify, cultivate, and support promising candidates with an interest in mission-driven institutions, especially from among deans and vice presidents at Catholic colleges and universities.

Unfortunately, a coordinated, comprehensive effort to prepare talented, committed individuals has yet to be established, although programs focused on orienting newly appointed leaders in Catholic higher education have emerged in recent years. It is not clear that these focused, short-term initiatives can meet the need for presidents able to foster the mission of Catholic higher education. Thus, a plan to identify and prepare individuals to be leaders in Catholic higher education must be developed and implemented.

Conclusion

The future of American Catholic higher education requires resolution of the four issues considered at BC's Sesquicentennial symposium. It is so evident that Catholic colleges and universities no longer exist in a closed environment where their Catholic mission and character can be presumed, where a broad consensus formed the religious attitudes and practices of the student body and most faculty, where the relationship of Church and university was not in question, and where well-prepared and formed leaders able to promote the college's Catholic mission and character were abundant. Catholic institutions of higher education now must develop strategies to deal with new challenges and opportunities.

In the next chapter, David J. O'Brien, Loyola Professor Emeritus of the College of the Holy Cross, provides an overview of how American Catholic higher education evolved since the 19th century. Essays by four experts follow: (1) Fr. Michael J. Himes, professor of theology at Boston College, "The Catholic Intellectual Tradition and Integral Humanism"; (2) Joseph A. Appleyard, S.J., professor emeritus, Boston College, "Student Formation in Catholic Colleges and Universities"; (3) Robert J. Kaslyn, S.J., dean of the School of Canon Law at The Catholic University of America, "'Catholic' as Descriptive of a University: A Canonical Perspective"; and (4) James L. Heft, S.M., Alton M. Brooks Professor of Religion and president of the Institute for Advanced Catholic Studies at the University of Southern California, "Leadership in

Catholic Higher Education." The final section contains a summary and concluding observations.

Appendix A includes the results of a survey of Catholic college presidents that preceded the symposium, and Appendix B lists the Catholic college and university presidents who participated in the symposium.

The History of American Catholic Higher Education

DAVID J. O'BRIEN

LOYOLA PROFESSOR EMERITUS, COLLEGE OF THE HOLY CROSS

E very college and university, including every Catholic college and university, has its own story. Those stories enrich present experience by reference to the past, and, given the ever-changing hopes of students, memories of alumni, and expectations of benefactors and friends, they are almost always stories with a trajectory toward the future. These are particular stories, about *this* place and *our* people. Higher education history is lived out not by all colleges and universities together but by individual institutions and communities. People know—and often love—their college or university; they are less engaged with the American, and in our case the Catholic, contexts within which their beloved institutions live and work.

Yet local historical narratives of colleges and universities often turn on presumptions about the past experience, current situation, and future prospects of America. And, in the case of Catholic colleges and universities, identifying stories cannot avoid presumptions about the historical trajectory of the American Catholic Church. These colleges and universities are what they are because they have been and are parts of American society and part of the American Catholic community. Their future will depend on how America and how the American Catholic community develops. For that future, they share responsibility, like it or not. Indeed, dialogue about the consequences of freely affirmed civic and religious, American and Catholic, commitments and responsibilities is at the heart of current debates about the mission and identity of American Catholicism. Arguments about the Catholic identity of American Catholic colleges and universities are simply one chapter in a larger and very important story of Catholicism and the American future.

Not long ago, being at once American and Catholic was not seen as a problem. When I graduated from the University of Notre Dame in 1960, as John F. Kennedy campaigned across America, President Dwight D. Eisenhower delivered the commencement address and Cardinal Montini of Milan, later Pope Paul VI, celebrated the baccalaureate Mass. We graduates knew and loved the Notre Dame success story revealed by the presence of such distinguished guests. We took it for granted that Notre Dame's story fit easily with our own Catholic and American family stories. "God, Country, Notre Dame," words chiseled over the entrance to Notre Dame's basilica, seemed a fitting banner for Catholic higher education as Catholics entered the American mainstream.

A half century later, Catholic universities prosper and enjoy remarkable popular support. They are confident that their research and teaching serves the common public good, and they hope that their work also serves the life and mission of the Church. But the American and Catholic stories are not what they were in 1960. There are differing American narratives, and American Catholic narratives, which are now matters of dispute, even of "culture wars," and that dispute has practical consequences for American Catholic higher education.[1] What does it mean today to be an American Catholic university? When priests and sisters led the institutions, staffed their offices, and taught in their classrooms, their identity was clear enough, at least on the surface. As we shall see, over the last 50 years that arrangement has changed radically, so that Catholic identity and integrity has become a central issue in every Catholic university and in all the stories they tell.

This essay is intended to be a contribution to that important conversation. *Conversation*, in this context, is a revealing word. The title of the now 20-year-old publication sent to all Jesuit college and university personnel to spark discussion of mission and identity, it is perhaps the most commonly heard word in local mission and identity programs—and it is one of those "practices" that does not fit easily with the now dominant narrative about American Catholic higher education.

---

[1]   Evidence of this is everywhere but I was particularly impressed with Michael Baxter, "God, Notre Dame, Country: Rethinking the Mission of Catholic Higher Education in the United States," delivered at the University of Dayton in 2011, where he makes impressive use of the arguments of Alisdair MacIntyre now found in *God, Philosophy, Universities* (Lanham, MD: Rowman and Littlefield, 2011).

History Happens

The overall history of Catholic higher education reflects the experience of American Catholics. Given the Protestant culture that dominated the United States, Catholics often decided to establish their own educational institutions. Until the 1950s most Catholic universities were led and staffed by priests, brothers, and women religious. The institutions had limited resources and little or no practice of faculty governance. Although they met accepted accreditation standards, few were academically distinguished and very few devoted significant resources to research and graduate education. Intellectual excellence was often subordinated to pastoral considerations. They limited their acceptance of many practices of American higher education, like academic tenure. Most maintained a central role for scholastic philosophy, "Catholic philosophy," in the curriculum.

All this has changed dramatically since the 1960s. The proportion of priest and religious on staff has declined, faculties are more professional (with doctoral degrees expected), tenure is widely granted, and faculty are more involved in academic governance. Independent boards of trustees are entrusted with responsibility not just for the schools' property, finances, and business practices, but for their mission. Many institutions stumbled financially for a while, but by the mid-1970s most prospered.

Today there is great diversity. Catholic universities vary in size and setting. Some have large endowments but many depend on annual enrollment. They differ in the student constituencies they serve, in their governance arrangements, and in their understanding of what it means to be a Catholic institution. Each of the 230 institutions—nearly 20 percent of all the Catholic colleges and universities in the world—is on its own, competing with others for students, faculty, and donors.

From the 1960s on, costs for faculty and staff rose rapidly, as did the expectations of students and parents. Meeting those expectations, responding to developments in local communities, keeping up with ever more complex public policies, and adjusting to dramatic changes in the Church all limited attention to the academic component of the schools' civic and religious responsibilities. Thus, in Catholic higher education, despite evident academic improvement and fiscal prosperity, the Catholic component of institutional mission and identity became at first uncertain, then contested.

The Story We Tell

American Catholic higher education finds its prevailing historical narrative in Philip Gleason's remarkable history, *Contending with Modernity*, and his many thoughtful essays about American Catholic academic life since Vatican II.[2] He shows that although Catholic universities arose from a bewildering variety of local initiatives and struggled for many years, they eventually prospered and lived out their mission and identity by pursuing some combination of three objectives.

First, they met the educational needs of aspiring Catholics, providing programs aimed at enabling persons to earn stable incomes, win respect from non-Catholics, and assist their families and local communities in the work of a democratic society. Catholic universities affirmed the drive of many immigrant Catholics to overcome discrimination and win a secure and respected place in American society.

Second, they met the Catholic community's need for clergy, religious, and lay leaders, providing pastoral care and philosophical and catechetic instruction aimed at strengthening Catholic religious practice and enriching the Catholic community. Arising from immigrant Catholic communities determined to preserve their cultural and religious heritage and from missionary efforts to preserve the faith in the new world, they were clearly Catholic.

Third, they met the needs of local communities for higher education, admitting applicants without religious restrictions (this was true in almost all cases), seeking support from local civic and social leaders, and providing services designed for local communities, in some cases demonstrating this civic commitment in their names—Boston College and the University of Dayton, for example. They later chose to participate in the professionalization of higher education by joining regional accrediting agencies and by demonstrating how their curriculum prepared students for admission to private or state university graduate and professional programs.[3]

As the universities developed after World War II and especially after Vatican II, while bishops and leaders of religious orders had pastoral objec-

---

[2] Philip Gleason, *Contending with Modernity: Catholic Higher Education in the Twentieth Century* (New York: Oxford University Press, 1995). Among his many essays on the subject, see in particular his Marianist Award Lecture, "What Made Catholic Identity a Problem?" (Dayton, OH: University of Dayton, 1994).

[3] Kathleen A. Mahoney, *Catholic Higher Education in Protestant America: The Jesuits and Harvard in the Age of the University* (Baltimore, MD: Johns Hopkins University Press, 2003).

tives, academic leaders hoped to live out their mission within and not apart from the wider academic community. That was not always easy, but doing so was required if they were to serve the aspirations of their students and their families. As the institutions grew, so did the number of serious scholars and energetic administrators, often impatient with the Church-focused priorities of their ecclesiastical superiors. At the same time, the universities benefited from the GI Bill as veterans could use their educational vouchers at Catholic institutions, thus opening a relationship with government, different from elementary and high schools. With this help, they responded to the needs of those and other students by expanding professional and business programs and gradually professionalizing their faculty and staffs.

Of course, from the start the institutions and those who led them were affirmatively and unapologetically American. At critical moments, as during the world wars, the Great Depression, and the civil rights challenges of the 1960s, they rushed to assist public mobilization. Their patriotic practices and daily work of teaching and research facilitated the "Americanization" of Catholics. The movement of many Catholics up the social and economic ladders and from outsiders to insiders was accompanied by the gradual integration of the universities into the rich diversity of American academic life. At the same time, Catholicism, once the religion of immigrant, working-class outsiders, was accepted as a full part of American religious pluralism.

Not surprisingly, this process of Americanization, fueled by popular aspirations, also contributed to the gradual erosion of the urban ethno-religious subcultures of Catholic parishes and neighborhoods. The historical location of the American Church, and thus the social basis of Catholic identity, was changing. Mission and identity would have to be renegotiated, everywhere.

Yet, as Gleason shows, for many years Americanization was not at the center of the story leaders of Catholic higher education told about themselves. They regularly insisted that the mission and identity of their institutions was found not in Americanist affirmations but in "contending with modernity," including American modernity. The papal condemnations of Americanism by Pope Leo XIII in 1899 and modernism by Pope Pius X a few years later called into question policies aimed at social acceptance, economic advancement, and shared civic responsibility.

Thus, leaders of Catholic higher education, while always affirming their civic loyalty, also emphasized how they provided a critical alternative to secular higher education. They helped the Church keep Catholics Catholic as they made their way into American democracy, with its perils to Catholic belief and morality. They did so by proudly announcing their Catholic identity: by encouraging an assertive, practical Catholicism marked by Mass attendance and pious practices; by centering on scholastic philosophy, known as Catholic philosophy, providing Catholic answers to pressing problems; by encouraging participation in "Catholic Action," works of service to the hierarchical apostolate; and by instituting the laity in Catholic social teaching.

This was the culture of Catholic higher education as it expanded dramatically after World War II. While deliberately Americanized, campus culture of these universities reflected the remarkable levels of sacramental practice, financial support, and religious vocations of the post–World War II American Church. The enthusiasm of Catholic academic leaders, proud of their own institutions, found expression in success stories like Notre Dame's, stories that turned on the larger success stories of America and its Catholic Church. Catholics were advancing in education, income, and social status and, happily, they were going to church, contributing money, and fostering vocations to the priesthood and religious life, all in record numbers.

Still, there were growing tensions between the "contending with modernity" understanding of mission and identity and the daily work of facilitating their students' entry into ordinary business, professional, and civic life. Professors at Notre Dame in my era liked to ask whether we were Americans who happened to be Catholic or Catholics who happened to be American. We often responded that it depended on where we stood as the question was asked. On the campaign trail with John Kennedy we might give the American answer. As we heard about the suffering Church in China and Eastern Europe and the medical-missionary work of Notre Dame graduate Tom Dooley and of the Holy Cross Fathers working in Bengal, we might give the Catholic answer.

As I graduated in 1960, we did not think much about the difference: that "Catholic *and* American" answer seemed to work. It provided us with a constructive, forward-looking vision of our American Catholic future. During the years that followed, which came to be known as "the long 1960s," experiences of racial injustice, the Vietnam War, the nuclear arms race, and abortion challenged our understanding of discipleship and citizenship.[4] Most simply,

---

[4] Historian Joseph Chinnici makes use of that frame for his developing history of the Vatican II and post–Vatican II American Church. See, for example, "Ecumenism, Civil Rights and the Vatican Council: The American Experience," *US Catholic Historian* 30 (Summer 2012), pp. 29–45.

it was no longer clear that what America required and what the Church expected fit snugly together. Thus, the question of identity in American Catholic higher education, then and now, turns on larger questions of the meaning of "American" and "Catholic" responsibilities, questions that are both personal and institutional, civic as well as religious.

Vatican II and Beyond

Gleason ended his history of American Catholic higher education at Vatican II (1962–1965). Alice Gallin, O.S.U., has documented the history of the period since. In *Independence and a New Partnership in Higher Education* (1996), she described the revolution of separate incorporation by which between 1967 and 1972 religious orders transferred ownership of and responsibility for their colleges and universities to independent boards of trustees.[5] In the famous *Land O'Lakes Statement* of 1967, leaders in Catholic education argued that authentic universities required "institutional autonomy" and academic freedom, yet theirs would remain fully Catholic by official profession, pastoral ministry, and the continued presence of the sponsoring religious community. Academic responsibility for maintaining the schools' Catholic identity would center on theology, once confined to the seminaries and unavailable to lay people, now brought on to the college and university campus and made central to the curriculum and intellectual life.[6]

The movement for separate incorporation and rapid professionalization arose from internal tensions between successful academic work and the extra-academic requirements made by the religious orders that owned the universities.[7] It was accelerated in the late 1960s and early 1970s by serious financial challenges and the prospect of governmental assistance open to

---

[5] Alice Gallin, O.S.U., *Independence and a New Partnership in Catholic Higher Education* (Notre Dame, IN: Notre Dame, 1996).

[6] Found in *American Catholic Higher Education: Essential Documents, 1967–1990*, edited by Alice Gallin, O.S.U. (Notre Dame, IN: Notre Dame, 1992).

[7] As she prepared her history of Catholic higher education since Vatican II, Sr. Alice invited Gleason and me to participate in a two-day interview with Theodore Hesburgh, C.S.C., Paul Reinert, S.J., and Ann Ida Gannon, B.V.M., the architects of separate incorporation and the first chairs of their new lay-dominated Boards of Trustees. Here they spoke of the tensions with religious superiors, the important resources provided by lay advisors, and pressing financial challenges. But they seemed less concerned with adapting to prevailing standards of academic practice than in shaping an engaged, responsible, and creative lay Catholic presence at the heart of American society. I am confident Gleason would agree with this assessment of their vision.

private higher education but unavailable to Church-related elementary and secondary schools. It was encouraged by the Second Vatican Council, which affirmed the autonomy of culture, the positive role of the laity in the life and work of the Church, and the need for Catholics to share responsibility with others for pressing historical challenges. Gallin finds in *Gaudium et Spes*, the Council's "Pastoral Constitution on the Church and the Modern World," the "Magna Carta of Catholic Higher Education."

Yet the Vatican never fully accepted the institutional autonomy of Catholic colleges and universities, believing that Catholic identity required some form of juridic accountability to the pastoral and teaching authority of the hierarchy. In the years following the Council, the Vatican insisted on exerting some control over Catholic theology, leading to periodic interventions by ecclesiastical officials. These were long dealt with informally through close cooperation of local bishops and college presidents and by a national "bishops and presidents committee." Under Pope John Paul II these discussions became more difficult, leading to the publication in 1990 of an Apostolic Constitution, *Ex Corde Ecclesiae*, with norms incorporated into canon law.

As executive director of the Association of Catholic Colleges and Universities from 1978 to 1992, Gallin played an important role in these discussions. In her history of the developments, *Negotiating Identity*, she shares with Philip Gleason the basic hermeneutic for this history: Americanization, which she places in the context of the theological discussion of "inculturation." The Catholic people after World War II went through a passage from the thick Catholic subculture of neighborhoods, parochial schools, extended ethnic families, and Catholic institutions whose Catholicism was pervasive and taken for granted. They moved toward and into the changing world of the American middle class and contemporary Catholicism with its internal diversities, fluid categories, and permeable boundaries. While all this was taking place, the country experienced serious social and political conflicts. At some point in the passage, Gleason and Gallin agree, Catholics lost a shared sense of what is meant for higher education by the word *Catholic*. This is what Gleason calls the "identity crisis" of Catholic higher education.[8]

The Vatican Council brought to American Catholics an invitation to the renewal of Christian vocation in the context of this Americanization passage from urban Catholic subcultures to the multiple centers of the expanding

---

[8] Gleason, *Contending with Modernity*, p. 318.

middle class. The fact that the invitation came amid the national and global challenges of the 1960s sharpened that experience of change and led many religious communities to place service to the human family as a whole at the center of their mission. And many of the institutions they served—hospitals, social service agencies, and colleges and universities—had public as well as ecclesiastical responsibilities and received government support and served the general public, further complicating the question of identity.

It is an important point: religious orders and their colleges and universities chose to accompany their people as they moved through that passage of Catholics from subcultures to the American mainstream, not to resist that passage as they had when they were "contending with modernity." As Gallin sees it, that choice was a pastoral response grounded in a sense of commitment to a specific people to help them find God, a response affirmed by the renewal following Vatican II. Others found in the same experience unacceptable accommodation to popular culture and secular standards, leading to a loss of Catholic identity and even integrity. The difference sometimes focused on higher education, but that debate was really about the experience of many of the Catholic people and the trajectory of U.S. Catholic history.

Gallin argued that pastoral accompaniment of the emerging middle class was also motivated by a shared Americanism: the freedom and opportunities for economic and social improvement that came with moving out of the Catholic subculture was a good thing for both the Church and the country. Gleason was far less optimistic about the historical trajectory of American Catholicism after Vatican II. He defended academic freedom and welcomed the growing investment in academic theology, but he worried that Catholic universities had suffered a loss of cohesion once associated with "Catholic philosophy" and he shared with another Notre Dame luminary, James Burtchaell, C.S.C., a concern about the distance that opened between Catholic higher education and the hierarchy.[9] As Gleason saw it, modern American Catholics, and Notre Dame, were in danger of abandoning the long Catholic campaign against modernity in favor of an ill-fated path of adaptation to secular society. He stated these concerns clearly and forcefully over many years, writing recently that *"Ecclesiastical authority"* (italics his) helped "stem what might have become an unintended slide into the kind of secularization

---

9   James Burtchaell, C.S.C., *The Dying of the Light: The Disengagement of Colleges and Universities from Their Christian Churches* (Grand Rapids, MI: Eerdmans, 1996).

experienced by Protestants a century ago."[10]

In recent years, many Catholic leaders have come to share Gleason's reservations about Americanization. In *Adapting to America: Catholics, Jesuits and Higher Education in the Twentieth Century*, William Leahy, S.J., emphasized a high degree of accommodation to American norms and practices.[11] He is less admiring than Gallin (or me) about recent history and regrets the failure of higher education leaders to be more self-conscious and more reflective and strategic about their shared responsibilities for the Church and the wider community. Moderates like Leahy think Catholics, not just colleges and universities, have overadapted and need to recover a sense of distinctive Catholic identity. This would mean emphasizing those Catholic qualities to set Catholics and their colleges and universities apart from their non-Catholic counterparts. Similar demands are made of Catholic hospitals and social service agencies, whose identities are thought to be similarly compromised by the professionalism and government entanglement that are part of Americanization.

In short, there is a now an all but consensual demand for more assertive expressions of Catholic identity in Church-related institutions. The dominant Catholic discourse and current ecclesiastical politics bend in the direction of resharpening the distinction between the Church and the world, in this case the American world. Identity is to be found in those things that make Catholics and Catholic institutions different, and central to those differences is commitment to the organized, institutional Church. All this is associated with a retold story of American Catholic history, which centers on the apparent loss of identity and threats to integrity arising from Americanization. To break out of these now chronic divisions will require development of another story, another historical narrative, about American Catholics.

Historical Narratives and Catholic Identity

This growing concern about identity echoes an earlier chapter in American Catholic history. In the 1890s the Vatican intervened to cut off a growing movement to encourage full participation by Catholics in American civic and

---

[10] Philip Gleason, "Through Many Dangers, Toils and Snares," Keynote Address, Conference on the Catholic University in the New Millennium, Notre Dame, 2005, copy kindly made available by Professor Gleason.

[11] William Leahy, S.J., *Adapting to America: Catholics, Jesuits and Higher Education in the Twentieth Century* (Washington, D.C.: Georgetown University Press, 1991).

cultural life. Dialogue about the relationship between Catholic and American values and practices was restricted and Catholics were encouraged to find religious meaning in the practice of the faith under the leadership of clergy and bishops. Then as now few noticed how these developments could drain the lay life of religious meaning and purpose. They resharpen the distance between clergy and laity, between the Eucharistic community shared with fellow Catholics and all those other relationships, networks, and associations that Vatican II said defined lay life. The laity, said *Lumen Gentium*, "by their very vocation, seek the Kingdom of God by engaging in temporal affairs and by ordering them according to the plan of God. They live in the world that is in each and all of the secular professions and occupations. They live in the ordinary circumstances of family and social life, from which the very web of their existence is woven."[12]

As the leaders of Chicago Catholic Action recognized a generation ago, emphasizing Catholic difference and distance from others makes lay Catholics less full disciples than they should or perhaps would like to be. It also means that Catholics are often outsiders, in opposition, in their country and its culture.[13] That has a powerful impact on the way one thinks about higher education and how one imagines what the life and work of graduates might mean in light of Christian faith. I would cite as examples by reference to two remarkable graduates of Catholic colleges, Catholic Worker Christopher Doucot, honored by Yale Divinity School with the annual William Sloane Coffin Award for Peace, and Leon Panetta, most recently director of the CIA and secretary of defense. Panetta was the featured lay speaker, with the Jesuit superior general, at an important convening of American Jesuit schools in 2000. The dominant loss of identity narrative would, if practiced, support the formation of prophetic outsiders like Catholic Workers, yet the practice of Catholic higher education favors the formation of responsible insiders like Panetta.

The now dominant narrative, critical of Americanization and insistent on affirming Catholic unity, orthodoxy, and distinctiveness, exists in some tension with central elements of academic practice. That narrative has indeed led to some course corrections. For example, it encouraged the growth of Catholic Studies, broadening the university's responsibility for Catholic intelligence

---

[12] *Lumen Gentium*, 31.

[13] See for example, the "Chicago Declaration of Christian Concern," with Commentaries in *Challenge to the Laity*, edited by Russell Barta (Huntington, IN: Our Sunday Visitor, 1980).

and imagination beyond theology, and helped to sharpen the critical edge of Catholic intellectual life on a whole range of important questions. But it makes it very hard to make Catholic identity an enriching element of core curriculum, particular disciplines, and business and professional studies. To achieve those goals, Catholic universities have developed a number of strategies, practices that stand in some tension with the dominant narrative. Those practices, it would seem, arise from another story about the history of American Catholicism and American Catholic higher education.

One practice is practical. Professors control the development and implementation of academic policy. Academic leaders, however insistent on Catholic mission and identity, quite properly want to avoid the sense that their university is a family firm where Catholics enjoy a privileged position. Instead, all faculty (and in another sense, staff) are invited to participate in and share responsibility for the mission of the university. This leads invariably to practical forms of Christian humanism, seeking common ground in the vocational commitments of the faculty, showing connections between those commitments and the mission of the university, and trusting that each and every person, Catholic or not, can and will support that mission and in the process express the institution's identity.[14]

Another practice is academic solidarity. In addition to the widely affirmed ecumenical and interfaith religious solidarity, and the social solidarity with the poor and the global human family, now consensual in the Church and its universities, there is also an intellectual solidarity. Some of the more heated rhetoric about Americanization (and secularization) suggests that the Catholic universities, and Catholic scholars, see their mission as providing an alternative to secular culture. In some areas of the world, especially where the faith is under siege, this may be true.

But it is far from the practice of American Catholic universities, where secular careers are launched and professional success is celebrated.[15] The institutions express their solidarity with others in higher education through a wide variety of national associations, while faculty and staff belong to professional

---

[14] A good example is found in *Engineering Education and Practice: Embracing a Catholic Vision*, edited by James L. Heft, S.M., and Kevin Hallinan (Notre Dame, IN: Notre Dame Press, 2011).

[15] Assumptions about secularization lay behind many of the criticisms of Catholic higher education and, more broadly, contemporary American Catholicism. For a wide-ranging discussion see "Theological Roundtable: Rethinking the Secular" in *Horizons* XXXV (Fall 2008), pp. 327–354.

associations and honor their standards. In these universities, research is properly valued within widely shared scholarly journals and networks, and teaching, including teaching about religious matters in the humanities, is enriched by cross-institutional collaboration. Scholarship, even theological scholarship, is carried on within and not apart from the general intellectual life. Catholic scholars of religion like Fr. James Heft, historians like James Turner, Leslie Tentler, and Scott Appleby, and theologians like Elizabeth Johnson, S.S.J., and David Hollenbach, S.J., provide vivid examples of such solidarity.[16]

A third academic practice that stands closer to a positive story of American Catholics and Catholic higher education could be called pastoral. In many academic communities persistent and ever-improving projects have aimed at sharing the charism of the founding religious order with faculty, staff, and students. One obvious example is celebration of "community," which has to do with respect for the dignity of persons and the importance of relationships. What the Jesuits call *cura personalis* is a valued element of Catholic academic life and whether it makes Catholic academic communities different from other academic communities seems not to matter.

Another example of pastoral care is the ongoing effort to help faculty and staff find a deeper meaning in their work, whether by reference to Catholic social teaching (for example, "the preferential option for the poor") or by engagement with Christian spirituality. Here powerful examples are provided by the ongoing adaption at Jesuit institutions of Ignatian spirituality to enrich the lives of faculty and students, Catholic or not, associated with the work of Howard Gray, S.J. Fr. Heft and his Marianist colleagues and other religious communities have similarly been able to use the resources of their religious order and the larger Church to help people turn careers into vocations. One could also note the remarkable 20-year work of Collegium with graduate students as well as faculty to connect faith and the academic vocation. On many campuses that I have visited, faculty and staff, many non-Catholics, testify to their grateful appropriation of the spiritual resources of their Catholic colleagues.

---

[16] Turner made this the basis of his work with the Erasmus Institute at Notre Dame, Appleby with the Fundamentalism Project and a decade of leadership in peace research. Hollenbach has made solidarity the center of one of the best essays on Catholic higher education in recent years. See "Catholic Higher Education Under the Sign of the Cross" in (among several other places and versions) *Finding God in All Things: Essays in Honor of Michael Buckley*, edited by Michael Himes (New York: Herder and Herder, 1996), pp. 279–298.

One could add to this list practices that stand at a remove from the dominant narrative of lost identity and threatened integrity. Academic governance aims to share responsibility by fostering the widest possible participation. Campus discussion of curriculum, while respectful of the need to ensure the availability of specifically Catholic resources, focuses attention on the needs of students and graduate students in an ever-changing national and global culture. Worries about overemphasis on career formation motivate defenses of liberal learning in which theology and religious studies participate. Successful business, professional, and civic leaders are honored and their assistance is sincerely solicited.

All these common practices find expression in the stories Catholic universities tell about themselves. They suggest the need for larger Catholic and American stories that provide a more positive understanding of the American and Catholic context of American Catholic higher education than is provided by what has become the standard narrative. That story invariably has a final chapter offering specifically Catholic prescriptions that will define Catholic identity, establishing countercultural differences with the surrounding culture and boundary-creating differences from other Americans. Such differences exist, of course, and all involved in Catholic life have a responsibility to nurture and support Catholic intelligence and imagination, but whether that work, apart from other good work, should be definitive of Catholic identity and Catholic mission is a serious question for Catholic academic communities and for all American Catholics.

I would argue that the American Catholic story is not one of over-accommodation to American culture requiring recovery of a countercultural identity. That formula will always deprive university work in business and the professions of authentic religious meaning. In fact, of course, American Catholics have been remarkably successful, and Catholic colleges and universities are filled with students who hope for the same opportunities. A more positive story of American Catholic liberation draws attention to those still seeking liberation and, equally important, to those who have achieved middle-class status and have the capacity to decide how they shall use their gifts without the ancient burdens of poverty and discrimination. To revise a liberal arts mantra: After liberation, how then shall we live?

In this liberation narrative, the last chapter gives historical meaning to decisions about social and civic life, work, and politics. Engagement with history, future as well as past, is the issue. Countercultural responses may make sense in some contexts—one thinks of John Paul II's Poland and Pinochet's Chile—but in the democratic American world such arguments giving priority to "identity" easily slip into denial of shared civic and cultural responsibility. Instead, orientation toward the future of everybody, inside and not apart from so-called secular society, our society, is central to a constructive understanding of the overall history of U.S. Catholicism. When the future is included, with the university as with most of us, the issue is one of solidarity, cited by popes as the central virtue needed in our age.

One consequence of the liberation story is well known: the need to "give back" by assisting others who seek liberation. This motivates universities' efforts to improve access, increase financial aid, and increase "diversity," and it shapes their impressive programs of community and public service. It also poses for them hard and far less recognized questions about the politics of knowledge and about university costs, access, and student debt.

And there is a second consequence: assisting those who have options and resources to work, indeed to live, for the building of what Martin Luther King, Jr., called "the beloved community." Much is done in Catholic higher education to provide students with knowledge and skills and an ethical framework, perhaps less to help them negotiate issues of work, career, and vocation, especially as these intersect with social and political responsibility. So we must consider the American side as well as the Catholic side of the mission and identity of the American Catholic college and university. We should aim to draw upon our faith, our Church, and our traditions to enrich our world at this moment in history and in that work renew and strengthen our identity. I think that is what solidarity requires.

The American Catholic story has been and remains a story of liberation, anticipated, desired, affirmed, and in some cases achieved. To the degree liberation is achieved, to that degree people, and their communities and institutions, become responsible for their society and culture. The response to countercultural arguments is that the culture is ours, and a part of ourselves. As we now have the capacity to decide for ourselves, shared responsibility for our country (our community of faith, and our culture) is a fact and not an option. The American Catholic story is not over. Together we are writing the next chapter.

The Catholic Intellectual Tradition and Integral Humanism

MICHAEL J. HIMES

PROFESSOR, THEOLOGY DEPARTMENT, BOSTON COLLEGE

S ome years ago I met a young woman who had graduated shortly before from a distinguished university and was beginning her professional career. She was preparing to enter the Catholic Church, and when I asked her why she had chosen to become a Catholic at a time when many of her contemporaries who were "born-Catholics" were leaving the Church, she replied that she was drawn to Catholicism by its insistence that she not compartmentalize her life. The refusal to allow us to divide our lives into separate and unrelated segments, the rejection of incoherence among the many aspects of human experience, is indeed a profoundly Catholic quality.

What I experience as a call to integrity of life, however, others regard as an act of religious aggression. This is often the case when there is question of the relation of religious belief and intellectual life—sometimes referred to as the conflict of faith and reason. Any attempt to establish a conversation between these two dimensions of human life is regarded with deep unease as an attempt of essentially irrational religious faith to set arbitrary bounds to intellectual inquiry and censor its conclusions. In such a context "Catholic intellectual tradition" seems an oxymoron.

That young woman who was attracted to Catholicism by its demand that she try to bring the various elements and abilities, actions and experiences, attainments and limitations of her life into a coherent vision of herself and the world recognized, I think correctly, that this is not an arrogant self-confidence that one has grasped the truth but rather a humble, ever-renewed hope that the truth has grasped you. Whether or not one thinks of that coherent world-view as an integrated system or an intelligible narrative, it is a whole in which all the parts fit. This truly Catholic perspective is always in process of achievement, never simply and finally possessed. The tradition of Catholic intellectual life is grounded in the fundamental Christian doctrine, the Incarnation.

Creation and Incarnation[1]

In order to explore the depth of the incarnational claim in the Christian tradition, another key symbol must first be explored: creation. However much they differ on the details, the two creation myths in Genesis (1:1-2:4a and 2:4b-25) agree on the central place that humanity occupies in the divine plan of the cosmos. In the first creation story, God is depicted as creating all things merely by speaking his command that they be (1:3, 6, 9, 14, 20, 24). On the afternoon of the sixth day, however, when God comes to the creation of human beings, for the first time God deliberates before the act of creation: "Let us make the human being in our image and likeness" (1:26). God has a model according to which the human being will be fashioned and the model is God's self. God confers on humanity dominion over all creatures: "Let the human being have dominion over the fish of the sea and the birds of the sky, the cattle, and all the wild animals, and all the creatures that creep upon the earth....God also said, 'See I give you for your food every seed-bearing plant on earth and every tree which bears fruit'" (1:26 and 29).

Three points should be noted in this first creation myth. First, creating human beings requires more planning and preparation than creating the firmament or separating the waters and the dry land or making plants and fish and birds and animals. Human beings are created last because their creation is the culmination of God's creative action. Humanity is God's masterpiece and has received God's fullest attention. Second, being human is the image and likeness of God. Third, since God has dominion over all creation, the

---

[1] Some of the following section is adapted from Michael J. Himes, "Catholicism as Integral Humanism: Christian Participation in Pluralistic Moral Education," in *The Challenge of Pluralism: Education, Politics and Values*, edited by F. Clark Power and Daniel K. Lapsley (Notre Dame, IN: University of Notre Dame Press, 1992), pp. 117–139, and from Michael J. Himes, "The Catholic Intellectual Tradition: Challenges and Resources," in *Examining the Catholic Intellectual Tradition*, vol. 2: *Issues and Perspectives*, edited by Anthony J. Cernera and Oliver J. Morgan (Fairfield, CT: Sacred Heart University Press, 2002), pp. 81–104.

creature that is like God must have dominion over all other creatures. Thus, humanity is given authority like God's and entrusted with the responsibility for what has been created.

The second creation myth reverses the order of events in the first. God fashions the first human being before plants and animals and fish and birds (2:7). All the rest of creation is designed to meet the human being's needs. Instead of being the culmination of creation, humanity is first in the order of creation, that for which everything else is created. The dominion over creation given to the human being is expressed in the divine permission for the human being to give names to all the other creatures, that is, to determine their nature (2:19-20). Both creation myths agree, however, that humanity occupies a unique place in the cosmos, that it is God's greatest work, and that everything else receives its purpose from its relationship to humanity. Humanity is the center of all creation.

But there is another point to be observed in the two creation stories in Genesis. According to the first, "God created the human being in God's image; in the divine image God created the human being, male and female God created them" (1:27). In this first creation myth, to be in the image of God means to be sexed. Sexuality means relatedness, incompleteness without the other. And that is part of being "like God," for God in the Hebrew Scriptures is always the God of the covenant, the God who is related to creatures. The notion of God "in God's self" is foreign to the Scriptures. The only God the Scriptures know is God in relation to creation. If being human is being "like God," then being human is being in relationship. The second myth makes this same point when God recognizes that "it is not good that the human beings should be alone" (2:18), and that there is no fit companion for a human being except another human being (2:22-23). Humanity is not "right" outside of community.

These two creation myths provide the context for the story of "the fall" and the introduction of evil into the divinely created cosmos. In the first of the creation stories the repeated divine judgment is that "God looked [at what God had made] and saw that it was good" (1:4, 10, 12, 18, 21, 25), and concludes with the statement that "God looked at everything that God had made and saw that it was very good" (1:31). The first temptation is to reject this judgment. The motive advanced by the serpent for disregarding the divine command not to eat the fruit of the tree of the knowledge of good and evil is that, if the first man and woman do so, they will "become like God in knowing good and evil"

(3:5).[2] The first creation myth, however, claimed that they are "like God," that God has created them "in God's image." The presupposition of the first temptation is that the divine judgment that human being is "very good" was false. The serpent invites the human being to deny that being human is being "like God" and so reject the goodness of humanity. The first sin is the acceptance of that invitation.

Thus, the origin of evil in the Genesis story of the fall is the denial that humanity is made in the image of God and the rejection of the goodness of being human. The entry of evil into the world that God had proclaimed good is the first human beings' loss of faith in the goodness of their existence. The first sin in this mythic account is neither disobedience nor pride; it is despair, the rejection of the goodness of finite, specifically human, being. And significantly, the first result of this sin is the collapse of relationship. The first man and woman now hide when God comes to stroll with them in the garden in the cool of the evening (3:8). The man who had greeted the woman with joyous recognition when he first encountered her (2:23) now blames her for having given him the forbidden fruit (3:12). The woman, in turn, places the blame on the serpent that she had trusted shortly before (3:13).

Human beings, who are only truly human in relationship with one another according to the creation stories, now turn on one another in mutual reproach. The erosion of trust and communion continues through the myths of prehistory in the first 11 chapters of Genesis. The fall story ends with human beings alienated from God. Shortly they become alienated one from another—the murder of Abel by Cain (4:1-15)—and then find themselves living in mutually alienated groups, symbolized by the collapse of communication—the tower of Babel story (11:1-9)—and the root of this ever-widening evil is the denial of the goodness of human being.

Against this background, the doctrine of the Incarnation can be seen as the startling claim it was intended to be. Perhaps its strongest statement is also one of the earliest, the hymn Paul quotes in the second chapter of the letter to the Philippians (2:6-11), a hymn presumably already known to the Christians

---

2   There is some ambiguity in v. 5. The word translated here as "God" is *elohim*, a plural form although used throughout the Hebrew Scriptures to refer to the one God. It is possible that the plural "gods" is intended here. If so, the phrase would be translated, "You will become like gods," i.e., celestial figures; see E.A. Speiser, *Genesis*, Anchor Bible (Garden City, NY: Doubleday, 1964), p. 23, note 6. In either case, the temptation is to reject the goodness of human being as it exists.

in Philippi. If the letter is authentically Pauline, it predates the composition of the gospels. Assuming the letter was written some time in the late '50s or very early '60s of the first Christian century and that the hymn quoted in it is earlier, this hymn could well be the earliest extant literary expression of the Christian community's faith concerning the person of Jesus, the now risen Christ (2:6-7).

> Although he was in the form of God,
> he did not think that being equal to God was something
>   to be held in grasp,
> but rather he emptied himself
> to assume the condition of a servant
> and became a human being
> and was like all other human beings.

This hymn has enormous importance for the Christian understanding of Christ, but its importance for Christian anthropology should not go unnoticed. When read against the background of the Hebrew Scriptures, it celebrates the archetype's having at last become one with the image. But this primitive Christian hymn states this in an extraordinary manner: the one who is in the form of God does not deem being Godlike as something to be retained but wills to become a human being exactly like all other human beings. This is the most sweeping claim concerning the goodness and dignity of creaturely being, and specifically of human being, which the Christian tradition has made: the Creator has chosen to become a creature, God has chosen to become a human being.

Nicholas Lash has written that "the real difficulty in saying the Christianity, or theology, is about God and man, the real difficulty in *verus Deus et verus homo*, consists not in knowing what we mean by *God* or what we mean by *man* (though these are no small questions), but in the difficulty of knowing what we mean by *and*."[3] Whatever "and" means in this christological usage, it does not mean "in addition." The classical Christian claim about Christ does not simply juxtapose divinity and humanity. Jesus of Nazareth is not divine "and also" human. The peculiar meaning of "and" in classical Christian

---

3   Nicholas Lash, *His Presence in the World: A Study in Eucharistic Worship and Theology* (London: Sheed and Ward, 1968), p. 4f.

doctrine might be rendered "in light of" or "because of." The doctrine asserts that in Jesus we see revealed true divinity insofar as we see true humanity, and that we see true humanity insofar as we see true divinity. The key to the understanding of classical christological doctrine is that divinity and full humanity are not in competition. The relationship between divinity and humanity revealed in the Incarnation is one of direct, not indirect proportion, i.e., the fuller the expression of God, the richer the humanity that receives the expression, *and* the more fully and richly human one is, then the more perfectly one receives God who is always self-gift.

This incarnational principle is closely connected to the symbol of creation. The religious significance of *creatio ex nihilo* is not only cosmological; it is also teleological, it makes a claim about the purpose of creation. Creation has no intrinsic ground. It gives nothing to God, not even glory. God needs nothing from creation. Therefore, the only reason for the existence of anything other than the Absolute Mystery that we name God can only be that God gives something to creation. But anything God would give to creation other than God's self would be part of creation. Creation exists so that it can be gifted, and the gift it is given is God's self. Everything that is exists so that God can communicate God's self to it. There is no other ground for being but the self-communication of God. Human being is that point in creation at which creation becomes capable of self-knowledge and self-acceptance, i.e., capable of recognizing the divine self-gift and accepting it gratefully. Humanity exists in order to be filled with the self-gift of God.

Pope's famous admonition, "Know then thyself, presume not God to scan;/The proper study of Mankind is Man,"[4] is correct, but not in the way he thought. For if the incarnational claim of Christianity is taken seriously, then to know human being is also to know God in part. Humanity exists in order to be the recipient of the self-giving of God. The exploration and development of the receiver leads to some grasp of the gift. Every creature, insofar as it is seen to be a creature, that is, to exist as the object of God's gift of self, is a sacrament, a symbol that by being what it is points to the presence of God. To know anything as created is to know it as referred to God. The ability of a thing to refer us to something else depends on our noticing it and appreciating that it is. The more a thing is, the more it refers. The primary requirement for being a religious symbol is simply being. A true religious

---

4   Alexander Pope, "An Essay on Man in Four Epistles," Epistle II, p. 1–2.

symbol does not stand for something else; it reveals that something else by being itself.

This is the true symbolism that, in the words of Goethe, "is where the particular represents the more general, not as a dream or a shadow, but as a living momentary revelation of the Inscrutable."[5] Goethe made this the crux of the distinction between poetry and allegory: the latter "seeks the particular for the general," whereas poetry "sees the general in the particular." The very nature of poetry is that "it expresses something particular, without thinking of the general or pointing to it."[6] If Goethe is correct—and surely he is no mean authority on poetry—then the Incarnation is the poetry of God. For the humanity of Jesus does not point to or stand for the fullness of the divine self-gift; that would reduce the Incarnation to allegory. It is by being fully, totally, and completely human that divinity is given expression—poetry of the highest order! If one is to symbolize God, one must be human; if one is to symbolize God so perfectly that one is God, then, that one must be perfectly human.

Not only are full divinity and full humanity not in competition, the latter is the symbol—or in classical Catholic terminology, the sacrament—of the former. The Catholic tradition maintains that the Absolute Mystery is never directly graspable, that the self-communication of God is always mediated, never immediate, that "no one can see the face of God and live" (Exodus 33:20). This is the sacramental principle that is so deeply rooted in Catholicism and so intimately related to the doctrines of Incarnation and creation. And the ultimate sacrament, the religious symbol that is always primary in the life of every human being, is the self. The discovery of the self in its intrinsic relatedness to other selves is the way in which we come to "know" God.

This incarnational base has grounded much of what has been richest in Christian theology from Augustine's insight that to speak of God he would first have to speak of the restlessness of his own heart to Karl Rahner's insistence that all theology begins with anthropology. For the human being has been created for the self-giving of God. In Rahner's term, the human being exists in order to be a "hearer of the Word": "We could now define man, within the framework of his supreme and darkest mystery, as that which

---

5   Johann Wolfgang von Goethe, quoted in Rene Wellek, *A History of Modern Criticism*, 2 vols. (New Haven, CT: Yale University Press, 1955), 1:211.

6   Ibid.

ensues when God's self-utterance, his Word, is given out lovingly into the void of god-less nothing."[7] Thus, recognizing that the Absolute Mystery that is God remains sovereignly *mystery* and so can never be adequately grasped in any human constructs or concepts, one can speak of the divine self-gift only by exploring that which is created precisely to be the recipient of the gift, the human person. In this sense, Rahner's claim is correct: "All theology is therefore eternally an anthropology."[8] To speak about God who is gift is to speak about the human being who is the object of the giving; to know the Word is to know the one who was called into being in order to hear the Word.

Integral Humanism

Taking this incarnational principle with maximal seriousness, it follows that the Christian life requires the fullest possible development of the human person in all aspects of his or her being. Integral Christianity is integral humanism. For if divinity and humanity are in direct, not indirect, proportion, then the more fully human one becomes, the more like God he or she becomes. Consequently, it is the duty of Christians who appreciate and believe in the radical import of the incarnational principle to work for the full humanization of all persons. Only by full humanization can human beings become more "like God," for God has not only created humanity in the divine image, God has become a human being "like us in all things but sin."

An obvious question must be posed: What is full humanization? How does one determine what constitutes integral humanism? Is not the point of so much dispute in our pluralistic society precisely the meaning of the term "human"? How then does the Catholic insistence on taking the incarnational principle with maximal import advance the discussion? And the plain truth is that it does not and cannot immediately answer these questions. What the Catholic tradition's incarnationalism and sacramentalism does do, however, is to make the question a religiously relevant one for believers. No Christian who gives to the Incarnation the weight that the Catholic strand within Christianity has given it can simply dismiss the concerns of humanism as mistaken or unimportant for his or her faith.

If humanity is what we share with God, which is certainly one of the impli-

---

7 Karl Rahner, "On the Theology of the Incarnation," *Theological Investigations* 4 (London: Darton, Longman and Todd, 1966), p. 116.

8 Ibid.

cations of the doctrine of the Incarnation, then as believers in the Incarnation, we must approach the question of the development of full humanity with nothing less than religious reverence. From the Alexandrian fathers of the second and third centuries with their interpretation of Christ as the *paidogos* of humanity and of Christianity as the ultimate stage of the divine paideia by which God leads creation to its full stature through the rise of the medieval universities to John Henry Newman's classic statement of the ideals of liberal education, *The Idea of a University*, the Catholic tradition has recognized the intimate connection between the Gospel and the process of humanization as that has been variously understood. Education, taken in its richest sense as the formation of the human person in the full and harmonious exercise of all his or her capacities, is a religious act for those who believe that humanity is what they and God have in common.

But what constitutes integral humanism is not answerable by Christianity alone. The claim that in Christ we see the one who is *verus Deus et verus homo* raises the question, as Nicholas Lash notes, of the meaning of "and" and sets guidelines for its answer, but it does not claim to resolve the questions of what we mean by God and what we mean by human.[9] The Christian tradition has something to say to both these questions, but it claims—or should claim— no final answer to either of them. Any attempt to insist on a final definition of God is blasphemous. And any attempt to insist on such a definition of the human person is, at best, presumptuous.

The first commandment of the Decalogue warns against idolatry, the besetting sin of religion (Exodus 20:3-5 and Deuteronomy 5:7-9). The temptation for religious persons and communities is always to identify God with their highest, purest, richest image of God. Deeply ingrained in the religious genius of the Hebrew tradition, to which Christianity is so much indebted, is its prohibition of all attempts to make an image of God. All images of God, all concepts of divinity, are in danger of becoming idols, for no image can be identified with God, no matter how traditionally sanctioned, scripturally based, doctrinally orthodox, or ecclesiastically approved. Idols must be smashed periodically: religious people must remind themselves that the "God" they imagine when they worship is not *God*.

Catholic theology has tried to be faithful to this anti-idolatrous principle of the Jewish and Christian traditions by maintaining that God is always

---

9   Lash, *His Presence in the World*, p. 4f.

Mystery. The absolute transcendence of God means that God can never be grasped in any conceptual formula or doctrinal definition. Such formulae and definitions may have something true to say about the Mystery, but they never exhaust it. Only God can express God's self perfectly, can speak a Word that is absolute self-expression to the point where Speaker and Word are one (John 1:1). If another is to hear that Word, that other must be fashioned by God to be an apt hearer of the Word. One typical way of expressing this is the prohibition of images "made by hands." For only God can make an image of God—and that image has been made: the human being.

The hallmark of true humanity for the Christian tradition, then, is its capacity to receive the self-communication of God. But that capacity presumes the ability of the human being to transcend and go beyond itself. It is the open-endedness of humanity, its capacity for self-transcendence, that makes the human person, the point in creation to which the divine self-communication can be made in an unsurpassable manner. It is this quality the doctrine of the Incarnation presumes. Thus, the one point regarding human being upon which Christianity must insist is precisely the inability finally and absolutely to limit human being. The very definition of the human person for Christianity is that it is the creature that cannot be defined. As the image of God in the hearer of the word, the human person is also mystery. Thus, the Catholic tradition within Christianity insists that the fostering of integral humanity means, first and foremost, that no preconceived limitations can be put on the meaning of humanity. Any form of humanism that imposes an absolute blueprint on the human person is not true or integral humanism.

At its best, the intellectual tradition of Catholicism recognizes that no formula, including none of its own formulae, can be made the final definition of true humanity. Catholicism should be—and sometimes is—*catholic*, that is, it acknowledges and respects other perspectives on the human person, so long as none makes pretensions to absoluteness. It realizes that no community of faith, however divinely founded, no tradition of thought, however rich, no strand of experience, however fruitful, can give a final answer to the question, "What is a human being?" Integral humanism, therefore, is open-ended and necessarily dialogic.

Absolute Mystery

In fidelity to its own deepest elements, therefore, Catholic Christianity should enter into free and open collaboration with all who seek full human develop-

ment, even when understandings of "human" differ. The Catholic intellectual tradition ought not to fear pluralism. Indeed, its commitment to the absoluteness of the mystery that is God and the transcendence of the human
person demands pluralism. Sadly, the Catholic tradition has not always been
consistent with its own deepest beliefs. As for all religious communities, idolatry has been a temptation for Catholicism and not always a successfully re-
sisted temptation. There have been occasions when the Catholic community
identified its notion of God with God, absolutized its dogmatic formulations
as immune to history, and elevated its practices to being the only genuinely
human life. When it has done so, it has suffered and caused others to suffer.

But at its best, Catholic Christianity embraces the relativizing of all doctrines, practices, and forms of worship that the acceptance of God as Mystery
entails. It then recognizes, in light of the incarnational principle, that to be
human is the way to be like God, and that the definition of the human is the
point in creation to which God communicates God's self. The Catholic intellectual tradition has deeply embedded within it—so deeply that it is sometimes forgotten—a central truth that must be taken with maximal seriousness: God is absolute Mystery.

All talk about God, if not idolatrous, is framed by two poles that I will char-
acterize by statements from Ludwig Wittgenstein and T.S. Eliot. Probably the
most frequently quoted sentence in 20th-century philosophy is the last propo-
sition of Wittgenstein's *Tractatus Logico-Philosophicus*: "What we cannot speak
about we must pass over in silence."[10] In other words, "If you don't know what
you are talking about, be quiet." This is an enormously important caution for
anyone who speaks about God, the incomprehensible Mystery that grounds
all that exists, for speech about mystery inevitably seeks to make it unmyste-
rious. We must be very cautious not to chatter on about ultimate Mystery as if
we know what we are talking about.

God demands reverent silence, as the Scriptures often remind us. Perhaps
the most dramatic instance of this is found at the climax of the Book of Job.
When Job, having refused to say that his suffering is the result of guilt he does
not feel, challenges Yahweh to come into court and explain himself, Yahweh
answers from the whirlwind in two powerful addresses, the most magnificent

[10] Ludwig Wittgenstein, *Tractatus Logico-Philosophicus*, translated by D.F. Pears and B.F. McGuiness, International Library of Philosophy and Scientific Method (London: Routledge and Kegan Paul, 1961), p. 151.

poetry in the Hebrew Scriptures. Yahweh hammers Job with a series of questions emphasizing the limits of human knowledge: "Where were you when I laid the earth's foundations?...Have you ever in your life given orders to the morning or sent the dawn to its post?...Have you visited the place where the snow is stored?...Can you fasten the harness of the Pleiades, or untie Orion's bands?" (Job 38:4, 12, 22, and 31).

In answer to the first of Yahweh's speeches, Job replies, "My words have been frivolous: what can I reply? I had better lay my hand over my mouth" (Job 40:4). The need for reverent silence is emphasized again in Job's response to the second of Yahweh's addresses: "I know that you are all-powerful: what you conceive, you can perform. I was the man who misrepresented your intentions with my ignorant words" (Job 42:2-3)." Laying one's hand over one's mouth when one is tempted to speak of mysteries that are too high, too incomprehensible for us, is a very Wittgensteinian pose. The first pole framing speech about God is the reminder that we do not know what we are talking about and that silence may well be the best response to Mystery.

But there is another pole. A quotation attributed to T.S. Eliot about poetry holds that there are some things about which we cannot say anything but before which we dare not stay silent. Some things are so important, so crucial to our own being, so necessary to our understanding of who we are and who others are and what the world is like, that we cannot be silent about them even though we know that whatever we say will be inadequate. Think of the words, "I love you." Has anyone ever said those words without the sinking feeling that they do not begin to convey what one feels? But silence is impossible. From Shakespeare's sonnets to woefully inadequate four-letter words sometimes used as synonyms for love in our society, we go on stuttering new ways to say, "I love you." They are all attempts to say what cannot finally be said. Yet we know that we cannot, indeed, that we dare not be silent.

Preeminently about God, who is not only ultimate Mystery but also the final destiny of all creation, it is impossible to remain silent. In speaking to undergraduates unenthusiastic about curricular requirements in theology, I often ask whether they think that their lives have purpose, meaning, direction, and if so, whether they produce that purpose, meaning, direction or, at least in part, discover it as already present. If they answer that they find meaning

---

[11] All translations are from *The New Jerusalem Bible* (Garden City, NY: Doubleday and Company, 1985).

present in their lives, I tell them that they are engaged in talking about God, even though they may never use the word. It is impossible to avoid God because God provides the meaning of our existence; it is impossible to be silent about God because it is impossible to be silent about the reality of purpose and meaning in our existence.

The religious use of language is carried on between these two poles. The danger for those of us who are professional talkers, "-ologists" in whatever "-ology" happens to be our specialization, is that all our speaking can mislead us into thinking that finally we know what we are speaking about. If we are speaking about incomprehensible Mystery, about God, then we need to be cautioned frequently about the inherent inadequacy of our expression and about the danger of glibness.

Of course, every theologian worth his or her salt has said this since time immemorial. No one has done so more rigorously than Thomas Aquinas, who insists that speaking equivocally about God tells us nothing and renders meaningful speech about God impossible, that speaking univocally about God is idolatrous, and that, therefore, we must speak of God analogically and so with enormous circumspection.[12] Nicholas Lash has suggested that the very definition of a theologian should be "someone who watches their language in the presence of God."[13] In words that I suspect Saint Thomas would have applauded, Lash writes, "Our words and thoughts concerning God are, indeed, inadequate but, as Newman knew, their inadequacy is acknowledged, their 'insufficiency' confessed, not by talking nonsense, but by talking carefully, by taking great care what we say."[14]

All our doctrinal statements are asymptotic. Like certain kinds of curves on a graph, they draw closer and closer to the axis but never intersect it—or, if they do, they intersect it only in infinity. We must profess our doctrinal beliefs with a bit more Wittgensteinian caution, with somewhat more of the spirit of Job before the whirlwind. One of the ways we can see this in the wisdom of the Church over the centuries is our traditional way of formulating doctrinal pronouncements: Let anyone who says thus and so be anathema. The doctrine teaches what cannot be said but not an absolutely final way in which

---

[12] *Summa theologiae* I, q. 13, a. 5.

[13] Nicholas Lash, "Reality, Wisdom and Delight," in his *The Beginning and the End of "Religion"* (Cambridge: Cambridge University Press, 1996), pp. 49–72 at 58.

[14] Ibid.

something must be said. Our doctrine has traditionally been phrased negatively and so avoided idolatry. We must constantly return to the incomprehensibility of God.[15]

The Intellectual Life Grounded in Love

The fundamental metaphor for the absolute Mystery that grounds all that exists is not truth; it is agapic love, self-gift. In his Oxford University sermons on faith and reason, John Henry Newman maintained that faith is a reasonable act albeit of a peculiar kind. Reason, he wrote, is a faculty of the mind by which we are brought to knowledge of what we cannot immediately know by our senses, "of gaining knowledge upon grounds given; and its exercise lies in asserting one thing, because of some other thing; and, when the exercise is conducted rightly, it leads to knowledge; when wrongly, to apparent knowledge, to opinion, and error."[16] If this is what "reason" is, he added, then "faith" is an act of reason. It may be an inadequate act, a badly performed act, carried through on mistaken grounds, but is surely an attempt to move from what is perceived to what is not.

Newman acknowledged that faith is often perceived as "weak" reason because it seems to jump to immense conclusions based on insufficient evidence. Either one must say that faith is faulty reasoning or that it is a form of reason that admits grounds that other forms of reason do not. As Newman put it, one must hold "Either that the process is illogical, or the subject-matter more or less special and recondite; the act of inference faulty, or the premisses [sic] underdeveloped; that Faith is weak, or that it is unearthly. Scripture says that it is unearthly, and the world says that it is weak."[17]

Faith is reason acting on different grounds than it usually does. Ordinarily, when people speak of reason, they mean "such inferences concerning facts, as are derived from the facts in question themselves, that is from Evidences, and

---

[15]   See the seminal articles by Karl Rahner, "Thomas Aquinas on the Incomprehensibility of God," in David Tracy, editor, *Celebrating the Medieval Heritage: A Colloquy on the Thought of Aquinas and Bonaventure, The Journal of Religion* 58 (1978) Supplement, pp. S107–S125, and "An Investigation of the Incomprehensibility of God in St Thomas Aquinas," in Karl Rahner, *Theological Studies, vol. 16: Experience of the Spirit: Source of Theology*, translated by David Morland (New York: Seabury Press, A Crossroad Book, 1979), pp. 244–254.

[16]   John Henry Newman, *Newman's University Sermons: Fifteen Sermons Preached before the University of Oxford 1826–1843* (London: SPCK, 1970), pp. 206–207.

[17]   Ibid., p. 208.

which lead consequently to Knowledge." Faith, by contrast, "begins with its own previous knowledge and opinions, advances and decides upon antecedent probabilities, that is, on grounds which do not reach so far as to touch precisely the desired conclusion, though they tend towards it, and may come very near it."[18] Newman summed up his attempt to define and distinguish faith and reason thus: "Faith, then, and Reason, are popularly contrasted with one another, Faith consisting of certain exercises of Reason which proceed mainly on presumption, and Reason of certain exercises which proceed mainly upon proof."[19] He might have noted that Pascal had written 200 years before that "the heart has its reasons of which reason knows nothing."[20]

Newman described faith as reason acting on what he called "presumptions," or "antecedent probabilities." His language is idiosyncratic, but his point is a familiar one. Augustine had held that faith was not a conclusion drawn from demonstrable premises. Faith arises from the restlessness of the heart driving us forward to the deepest level of our desire. Thomas Aquinas had taught the knowledge that God exists is rooted in us by nature in a general and confused way because God is our happiness.[21] This presumptive knowledge of God rests not on objective evidence; instead, we arrive at such evidence precisely because we have been rendered sensitive to it by our desire for what it points us toward. So, Thomas taught in treating the question whether some see God more perfectly than others, the mind must be made "deiform," which I translate as "God-shaped," in order to know God, and this deiformity is the result of the light of glory.

Those who see God more perfectly participate in this light of glory more fully, and those who participate in the light of glory more fully love more. "For where there is greater love [*caritas*] there is greater desire, and in a particular fashion desire makes the one desiring more apt and ready to receive what is desired."[22] Or, as W.H. Auden put it, "the first criterion of success in any human activity, the necessary preliminary, whether to scientific discovery or to

---

[18]   Ibid., p. 223f.

[19]   Ibid., p. 223.

[20]   Blaise Pascal, *Pensées*, trans. by A.J. Krailsheimer (London: Penguin Books, 1966), p. 154 (#423).

[21]   *Summa theologiae* I, q. 2, a. 2, ad primum.

[22]   *Summa theologiae* I, q. 12, a. 6, resp.

artistic vision, is intensity of attention or, less pompously, love."[23] The Catholic intellectual tradition is rooted in love of the truth. It is not about the acquisition of knowledge; it is about awed delight in being. It is about coming to agree with God's judgment on all that exists: God looked at it and saw that it was good (Gen 1:4).

---

[23] W.H. Auden, "A Review of The Book of Talbot, by Violet Clifton," in *The Complete Works of W.H. Auden, Prose*, vol. 1: 1926–1938, edited by Edward Mendelson (Princeton, NJ: Princeton University Press, 1996), p. 43.

Student Formation in Catholic Colleges and Universities

J.A. APPLEYARD, S.J.

PROFESSOR EMERITUS, BOSTON COLLEGE

A ll colleges form their students. The campus—its classrooms, faculty and administrative offices, residence halls, dining rooms, chapels, and play- ing fields—is the principal setting for four critical years of their development as human beings. The shape of this development is not automatic and inevi- table; common sense tells us it needs to be supported and facilitated. If so, is it guided by a coherent vision of what this development entails? And who is responsible for implementing this vision? These questions are at the heart of any consideration of student formation.

Let us take for granted that intellectual formation is the primary goal of a college education and that social formation—the process of composing a coherent sense of identity in meaningful relationship to others and to com- munities of value—is also a desirable outcome. Where agreement tends to fall apart, however, is when intentional moral and religious formation is pro- posed as a suitable goal of a college education, though for much of the history of American higher education it was the norm. An adequate concept of stu- dent formation, I suggest, regards all these kinds of formation as desirable, as interconnected and integrated, and as the responsibility of all the adults who have a role in students' education.

Is this view of formation imaginable today, even in Catholic colleges and universities? Two stories provide the historical background for answering this question. The first helps us understand how the forces that transformed American colleges and universities at the end of the 19th century marginal- ized religious and moral formation and are still determining how much of higher education thinks about student formation. The second helps us understand why Catholic higher education sustained a strong devotion to a more complete student formation until well into the 1960s and why, though it almost lost sight of this purpose in the effort to be evaluated by mainstream academe's measurements of excellence, it persists in regarding formation as a central, if not always well-understood, dimension of its mission.[1]

The Evolution of Student Formation in the American College

From the founding of Harvard in 1636 until well into the 19th century, there was a widely shared agreement that the purpose of a college education included the intellectual, social, and moral formation of students, and that religion was an unquestioned component of this formation.[2] The earliest document describing Harvard's educational philosophy says:

> Let every Student be plainly instructed, and earnestly pressed to
> consider well, the main end of his life and studies is, to know
> God and Jesus Christ which is eternal life, John. 17.3, and there-
> fore to lay Christ in the bottom, as the only foundation of all
> found knowledge and learning. And seeing the Lord only giveth
> wisdom, let every one seriously set himself by prayer in secret to
> seek it of him, Prov.2.3[3]

This lofty purpose was supported by a classical curriculum (Latin, Greek, Hebrew, Scripture, Christian doctrine, history, some mathematics and science) and by the structure of residential college life: a highly regulated daily order, chapel services, character-building discipline, and a largely clerical faculty.

Agreement about the curriculum soon fragmented, for several reasons.

---

[1] Other religious denominations, especially Protestants, sponsor colleges that have maintained in varying degrees a visible religious identity. I do not intend to take their situation into account here because the issues they face in forming their students are not fundamentally different from those of Catholic institutions.

[2] This overview of early education in the colonies is drawn from Frederick Rudolph's *The American College and University: A History* (Athens, GA: University of Georgia Press, 1962, 1990) and his *Curriculum: A History of the American Undergraduate Course of Study Since 1636* (San Francisco: Jossey-Bass, 1977).

[3] Samuel Eliot Morrison, *The Founding of Harvard College* (Cambridge, MA: Harvard University Press, 1935), p. 434.

New knowledge, especially in the sciences and mathematics, constantly arrived from Europe and progressive teachers wanted to make room for it in the curriculum. Parents and students demanded that useful subjects—book-keeping, engineering, and so forth—be taught alongside the classical subjects. Economic growth gave new opportunities to an expanding population and created demand for practical courses of study. When in 1861 the federal government gave income from the sale of Western lands to each state to support public education, new institutions multiplied, devoted to programs that matched local needs like agriculture, dairying, mining, and forestry. The legacy of the Civil War called into question the pretensions of the classical curriculum to offer a useful consensus of religious and philosophical wisdom.

Even more significant was the new concept of university that emerged in Germany in the later decades of the 19th century, emphasizing the empirical study of data, recovering and editing texts, and understanding historical contexts and influences. Instead of refining and transmitting unchanging truth, the role of faculty became discovering and disseminating new knowledge. Once generalists, they became specialists. Institutions divided their faculties into departments devoted to specific disciplines. Professional scholarly associations sprang into being, creating bodies of scholarly authority independent of received tradition.

When in 1885 Harvard's president endorsed the idea that students should be allowed to take any courses the college offered in any order they pleased, he said that Harvard was recognizing that "a young man of nineteen or twenty ought to know what he likes best and is most fit for."[4] He might more aptly have said Harvard was recognizing that faculty should be able to teach what they were interested in. In 1870, Harvard had 32 professors teaching 73 courses; by 1910, 169 professors and twice that many instructors of lower rank taught 401 courses.[5] Soon professional schools in law, medicine, business, education, nursing, divinity, and other subjects were being established within universities, transforming what had previously been "intern" forms of professional training or separate training institutions into academic programs for advanced degrees.

In the new role the university found for itself, supplying graduate and professional programs for a growing industrial society—programs staffed by

---

[4]   Rudolph, *American College*, p. 292.

[5]   Rudolph, *Curriculum*, p. 206.

faculty trained in specialized scientific inquiry—the classical outlook and the generalist orientation of the clerically controlled liberal arts colleges looked amateur and out of date. Moreover, the new empirical disciplines seemed to discredit the intellectual foundations of biblical religion and the moral system grounded in it, and for many reform came to mean freeing colleges from clerical control. These developments did not grow out of any principled antagonism toward Christianity, historian George Marsden points out. They were promoted in the name of a broader, more open Christianity that was taking its cultural responsibilities more seriously. He quotes the striking 1866 remark of Frederic Henry Hedge, a Unitarian minister and professor at Harvard Divinity School: "The secularization of the College is no violation of its motto, '*Christo et Ecclesiae.*' For, as I interpret those sacred ideas, the cause of Christ and the Church is advanced by whatever liberalizes and enriches and enlarges the mind."[6]

But liberal Protestantism made a fatal choice, Marsden argues, in allying itself with the view that scholarly objectivity required the suspension of religious beliefs. In doing so, it acknowledged the acceptability of a methodological secularism that accepted as normative for the intellectual life a sharp division of labor between scientific activity and theological and moral speculation. They might illuminate each other, and for the devout Christian suggest a higher unity of knowledge, but henceforth the ideal of scientific inquiry free of any religious presuppositions would be the major operative standard in the new academic fields and the new university.

Traditional Christianity did not disappear from the university overnight. The later 19th century was the era of strong evangelical piety and the "Social Gospel," which valued the kind of "volunteer Christianity" demonstrated by attending chapel services, joining religious study groups, and working in settlement houses, the YMCA, and other programs that served social needs. Curiously, one curricular development even consciously preserved a residue of Christian humanism. The historicist and evolutionist mentalities embodied in the new approach to scholarship allowed the claim that a reliable foundation for moral and spiritual values could be located in the evolution of Western culture itself. As a result, the 1920s saw the widespread adoption of "Western Civilization" humanities courses. In effect, Western culture and

---

6   George M. Marsden, *The Soul of the American University: From Protestant Establishment to Established Nonbelief* (New York: Oxford University Press, 1994), p. 186.

the humanities embodying it replaced traditional Christianity as a vehicle for teaching liberal moral and cultural values in the American college and university.

In practice, this meant that, from the 1920s until the 1960s, the teaching and study of the natural and social sciences and the other scholarly disciplines would be governed by positivist empirical methods, while—even in public institutions—traditional religious and moral values would be conveyed by study of the humanities and the liberal arts. This was explicitly stated in Harvard's influential 1945 report *General Education in a Free Society*. It recognized that "a supreme need of American education is for a unifying purpose and idea," and it found that unifying ideal in the humane tradition of the West, frankly acknowledging that "education in the great books can be looked at as a secular continuation of the spirit of Protestantism."[7]

One further development needs to be mentioned: the growth of the "extra-curriculum" as a de facto form of student formation and the appearance of student-personnel administrators with a special responsibility for furthering students' well-being or at least monitoring their behavior. In the evolution of the American college students, college administrators have persistently vied for control of the student experience. One of the earliest forms student independence took was the establishment of debating or literary societies, free from administrative supervision, which grew to such prominence that in the 1840s some literary societies possessed libraries superior to the colleges' own collections. Here students could read what they wanted in fields the curriculum didn't cover (such as vernacular literature, history, contemporary science, and current affairs) and could relax, smoke, and drink.

Another form was the fraternity (and later sorority) movement. The earliest versions, at liberal arts colleges like Amherst, Williams, and Brown, and parallel entities such as Princeton's eating clubs, were settings where students could develop the social, artistic, and political sides of their personalities, which college administrations of the time had little interest in cultivating. Athletics were another form of this extracurriculum: first gymnastics, boating, and similar entertainments on a modest scale, then intercollegiate team sports on an increasingly grander scale.

---

[7] George M. Marsden, "The Soul of the American University: An Historical Overview," in *The Secularization of the Academy*, edited by George M. Marsden and Bradley J. Longfield (New York: Oxford University Press, 1992), p. 23.

Both forms eventually moved back onto campuses as student energy and creativity blossomed into the musical societies, dramatic groups, magazines, and newspapers we now think of as student "activities."

By the end of the 19th century, a number of these developments—the fraying agreement about the religious and moral principles that should guide a college's purpose, the increasing diversion of faculty attention to specialized research, the multiplication of curricular options available to students and the necessity of finding one's path among them, and the burgeoning of extracurricular options competing for students' interest—created the need for a new class of administrators to deal with student life and the challenges it presented, both to students and to the institution.[8] Harvard seems to have appointed the first student dean in 1890 and other colleges soon followed.

The role might be vague—at George Washington University it was described as "helping the student to get hold of life, to find the right environment in which he can develop himself to his fullest capacity"—but in general, deans of men (and soon of women) were concerned with the whole student, administering discipline and offering advice about how to navigate the complexities of college life and growing up. The emerging field of psychology had a significant influence on the work of student life administrators, as it produced specialists in measurement and testing, vocational advising, and mental health. A new term appeared in the vocabulary of college administrators to describe those who dealt with "personnel" and in 1919 NASPA, the National Association of Student-Personnel Administrators, was founded.

This movement is significant as a marker in the gradual redefinition of responsibility for whatever kind of student formation was happening. In 1937, a group of NASPA administrators set out the principles of this new profession in *The Student Personnel Point of View*. Influenced by John Dewey's humanist philosophy of the person, they proposed that one of the basic purposes of higher education is to assist the student in developing to the limits of his potential, only a part of which would be his intellectual development.

> This philosophy imposes upon educational institutions the obligation to consider the student as a whole—his intellectual capacity and achievement, his emotional make-up, his physical condition,

---

[8] James J. Rhatigan provides a succinct history in "From the People Up: A Brief History of Student Affairs Administration," in *The Handbook of Student Affairs Administration*, edited by George S. McClellan et al. (San Francisco: Jossey-Bass, third edition, 2009), pp. 3–16.

his social relationships, his vocational aptitudes and skills, his moral and religious values, his economic resources, and his aesthetic appreciation. It puts emphasis, in brief, upon the development of the student as a person rather than upon his intellectual training alone.[9]

The statement confidently asserts a new division of responsibility for the student's education. The faculty will oversee intellectual formation. Social and moral formation will be the work of student-affairs professionals. The agreement has held, for better or worse. Interestingly, the 1937 document listed among possible student personnel services: "Supervising, evaluating, and developing the religious life and interests of students."

With the huge growth of colleges and universities in the years after World War II, and the large infusions of government money, secular American higher education sorted out into two broad categories. The elite institutions that had grown out of the older liberal arts colleges—even those like Harvard that became behemoths of scientific research and professional education—continued to sustain a nominal humanistic tradition. The rapidly expanding public systems, on the other hand, though they offered elements of a general education for the humane values it encouraged, understood that their mission was educating citizens for the professional roles they would play in a democratic, technologically triumphant society.

A chorus of prominent critics has recently raised their voices in protest against this arrangement, in elite institutions especially: Harry Lewis, a former dean of Harvard College, Anthony Kronman at Yale, Martha Nussbaum at the University of Chicago, and most recently Andrew Delbanco at Columbia University. The titles of two of their books succinctly convey their argument: Lewis's *Excellence Without a Soul: How a Great University Forgot Education* and Kronman's *Education's End: Why Our Colleges and Universities Have Given Up on the Meaning of Life*.[10] Lewis puts the charge this way: universities today

---

[9]   Ibid., p. 11.

[10]   Harry Lewis, *Excellence without a Soul: How a Great University Forgot Education* (New York: Public Affairs, 2006) and Anthony T. Kronman, *Education's End: Why Our Colleges and Universities Have Given Up on the Meaning of Life* (New Haven, CT: Yale University Press, 2007). The titles of Nussbaum's and Delbanco's books are *Not for Profit: Why Democracy Needs the Humanities* (Princeton, NJ: Princeton University Press, 2010) and *College: What It Was, Is, and Should Be* (Princeton, NJ: Princeton University Press, 2012).

succeed better than ever as creators and repositories of knowledge, but they have forgotten that the fundamental job of undergraduate education is to help students to "grow up, to learn who they are, to search for a larger purpose for their lives, and to leave college as better human beings."[11] Overemphasis on research and on training students for professional lives has marginalized the project of liberal education to the point where it has all but disappeared.

When these writers describe what they mean by "the meaning of life," they tend to speak of "democratic values" or "civic virtue" or being "fully human beings." They see no role for religious belief or religious perspectives in rectifying the shortcomings they identify. If mentioned at all, religious beliefs are simply, at best, among the values that might play a role in a student's thinking and therefore need to be examined critically. These books handily illustrate Marsden's comment that in the contemporary university religion is about as important as the baseball team.[12]

Student Formation in Catholic Colleges and Universities

The Catholic story has a significantly different plot. Though Georgetown traces its beginnings to 1789, few Catholic colleges existed until the 1840s.[13] But from that time religious orders and sometimes dioceses founded colleges by the dozens in every decade until World War II, the Civil War years excepted. Though only a third of these survived, those that did followed much the same pattern of growth and change as their private and public peers. The religious orders and clergy who came to the young republic from Europe shared the conviction of their Protestant predecessors that establishing schools was a way of planting the faith and supporting its growth, preparing candidates for the clergy, and giving young men (and eventually women) the skills and the social polish they would need to enter adult life and responsibilities with the support of a strong religious faith.

The classical curriculum based on Greek and Latin languages and literature, supplemented by mathematics, history, geography, and modern languages such as French and Spanish, usually held a place of honor in the prospectus of a Catholic college. One of the earliest adaptations in almost all institutions

---

[11] Lewis, ibid., p. xii.

[12] Marsden, *Secularization*, p. 33.

[13] I am drawing here mainly on Edward J. Power, *A History of Catholic Higher Education in the United States* (Milwaukee: Bruce Publishing Company, 1958).

was to add as an option an "English course" alongside Greek and Latin and later scientific and commercial courses. One mother wrote to the president of Holy Cross in 1848 about her son's studies: "Let him apply himself to English grammar, geography and arithmetic...they will be more useful to him than any others as he will probably be sent to a trade in a year or two."[14]

What made all these subjects suitable for moral and religious instruction was the pedagogy that was traditional in European Catholic schools, which found spiritual and ethical lessons in the stories students read, the historical characters they encountered, and even the scientific information they acquired. Curriculum and pedagogy were strongly supported by the practices of school life—regular celebration of Mass and the sacraments, prayers throughout the day, seasonal celebration of Church feasts and of saints especially proposed for emulation, student activities such as sodalities to encourage competitive devotion—and of course a largely clerical body of teachers. Since most colleges were directed by religious orders and were small boarding institutions where teachers lived with students, pervasive control of the institutional culture for its formative purposes was the norm.

Two factors shored up the Catholic colleges' strong sense of identity and preserved until well into the 20th century their commitment to an ethos of deliberate religious and moral as well as intellectual formation of students. One was the social and political experience of the American Catholic community, especially in the large urban centers of the East and the Midwest, where Catholics, outsiders to the dominant Protestant culture, struggled for a share of political and economic power. The policies of Church leaders encouraged the formation of separate Catholic social and professional organizations. Parish life, with its sacramental rituals, novenas, sodalities, and Latin language, further reinforced the distinctiveness of the Catholic community and its self-sustaining inward focus. The extensive system of primary and secondary Catholic schools readily transmitted this culture onward into the colleges.

The second and perhaps more important factor was the late-19th-century revival of scholastic philosophy and its endorsement as the all-but-official intellectual perspective of the Church by Leo XIII in the encyclical *Aeterni Patris* in 1879. Basically Aristotelian realism brought into harmony with Christian revelation by Thomas Aquinas in the 13th century, it understood God as the author of truth in both realms and the human person as able to attain

---

[14] Ibid., p. 56.

objectively true knowledge of reality—including the natural law imprinted in the human heart and expressed in the voice of conscience—and, with free will, able to choose between alternatives apprehended by the intellect.[15]

The Thomistic system appealed to educators both as a counterweight to skeptical modernity and as a philosophy of education for Catholic youth. Very quickly, it became the integrating capstone of the curriculum in American Catholic colleges and universities. In 1900, for example, Georgetown required nine courses spread over junior and senior years: logic, epistemology, metaphysics, cosmology, history of philosophy, psychology, natural theology, and general and special ethics.[16] In effect, a student majored in scholastic philosophy, whatever else he was studying. Undergraduates at Boston College in the 1950s were taking almost the same set of courses. Curiously, theology played a minor role in the presentation of the Thomistic synthesis. "Religion" courses were required, but as a kind of higher-level catechism, not as a subject for speculative exploration.

The practical usefulness of neo-scholastic philosophy was demonstrated in the encyclicals of Leo XIII in 1891 and Pius XI in 1931, which set out a vision of a social order guided by principles such as the dignity of all people, their solidarity with one another in pursuing the common good, the subsidiarity of functions within the community, the right to a just share in the fruits of economic gain, and the duty of caring for the needy. The curriculums reflected these developments and graduated students conversant with and largely sympathetic to these ideas. For many young Catholics who joined progressive organizations such as the Catholic Worker Movement in the years between the World Wars, scholasticism's vision of a culture grounded in both faith and reason provided the building blocks of a forward-looking social and political program compelling enough to change their lives.

The high point of American Catholic culture, in terms of its cohesiveness, reach, self-confidence, and internal authority, may have been the decades before and after World War II. Catholic colleges and universities, reflecting this confidence and energy, grew dramatically in the postwar period and were determined to be judged by the same standards as their secular peers. They

---

[15] Philip Gleason, *Contending with Modernity: Catholic Higher Education in the Twentieth Century* (New York: Oxford University Press, 1995), pp. 116–118.

[16] John B. Brough, "Philosophy at Georgetown University," in *Georgetown at Two Hundred*, edited by William C. McFadden (Washington, D.C.: Georgetown University Press, 1990), p. 115.

multiplied graduate and professional degree programs, competed for better students, raised standards for faculty hiring, evaluated the scholarly productivity of those hired, recruited student-life administrators from top programs, professionalized their administrations, and grew their endowments. Accrediting associations welcomed them as exemplary neighbors.

Interestingly, considerable data show how successful Catholic colleges and universities of this period were in providing a specifically Catholic formation for their students. Sociologist Andrew Greeley, then at the beginning of his career, set out in 1961 with colleagues at the National Opinion Research Center at the University of Chicago to provide empirical data about the state of American Catholic higher education. They were surprised to discover that Catholics were no different from other Americans in college—they were as likely to enroll in graduate studies, to plan on a career in college teaching or research, to be studying in the top-ranked universities and doing well academically there—and they showed no signs of defecting from their faith in the secular atmosphere of graduate schools. Moreover, those who went to Catholic colleges were more likely to remain in the Church, to attend church weekly, and to have married a fellow Catholic. On various indices of religious attitudes and practice (sacramental reception, regarding the Church as teacher, ethical orthodoxy, doctrinal orthodoxy, religious knowledge, and attending Mass more than once a week), they scored notably higher than Catholics who did not attend Catholic colleges. And they scored lower on indices of anti-Semitism, anti-civil liberties, and religious-extremism indices, and about the same on racism and community-involvement indices.[17]

Seven years later, Greeley again studied the graduates of 1961 and concluded that the graduate of a Catholic college was somewhat more liberal, politically and socially, than Americans at large; somewhat more successful, economically and academically; still a practicing Catholic; more likely to be loyal to his school; and more likely to be satisfied both with what the institution tried to accomplish and with what, in fact, it did accomplish in his educational experience. And, he notes, more likely to say that religious education is an important factor in seeking a college for his children, and indeed that it would be important for his child to attend the same college he did.[18] All in all, not a bad

[17] Andrew M. Greeley, *From Backwater to Mainstream: A Profile of Catholic Higher Education* (New York: McGraw-Hill, 1969), pp. 85–98.

[18] Ibid., pp. 99–108.

record of accomplishment for Catholic higher education in 1961.

Greeley's reassurance was paradoxical in its timing, however. When his book appeared in 1969, the American cultural consensus and the golden age of Catholic America were already on the verge of collapse, along with the confidence of Catholic higher education in its identity, methods, and tradition. Alice Gallin's *Negotiating Identity* and the final chapters of Philip Gleason's *Contending with Modernity* are excellent starting points for anyone trying to make sense of this period. Here I just want to point to two of the major factors that affected student life in Catholic colleges and universities.

One factor was the American cultural explosion of the '60s and '70s, which undermined so much of American institutional life. The other factor was Vatican II, the Catholic Church's own experience of upheaval. Both sets of events reverberated on campuses. Student discipline withered, dress codes disappeared, rules separating men and women in residence halls weakened, required attendance at Mass was unimaginable. The civil rights and antiwar movements empowered campus activists. Protests, building takeovers, and strikes became commonplace. Philosophy and theology requirements were a regular target and most Catholic colleges and universities drastically reduced theirs, some even eliminating their whole core curriculums. In the years of expansion and improvement in institutional standing, faculty and staff had been hired with an eye more to their professional accomplishments than to their familiarity with and interest in the Catholic mission of the institution; now, when policy issues were at issue, it became far less clear how to draw on an agreed Catholic identity. Catholicism, which in the past had defined and symbolized the distinctive character of the institution, often became a point of polarity and debate.

In some ways, the most dramatic change was the abandonment, almost overnight, of the neo-scholastic philosophy program, a system that had seemed to embody the heart of Catholic intellectual life. Looking back, reasons are not hard to find: the courses required good teachers, which were not always easy to hire in the postwar expansion years; students found much of it a dry and abstract system unrelated to real experience; it put a premium on mastering formulas and was taught out of textbooks that digested the ideas of Descartes, Kant, Marx, and other "adversaries" into spoonfuls; and younger faculty who had studied in Europe were often more interested in phenomenological and existential currents of thought and didn't buy into the claim that neo-scholasticism offered a privileged unifying Catholic view of life. We can't discount as well the reality that the philosophy curriculum was a large and available target for antiauthority sentiment and the demand for change.

Were the dramatic changes of the '60s and the '70s loss or gain? Did Catholic higher education succumb to the values of a secular culture, as some critics have said, or were these developments the stirrings of healthy change from within, pointing institutions to a sounder integration of academic excellence, faith, and meaningful engagement with society? Much depends on how these questions would be answered in the years that followed.

In 1968, in a wide-ranging survey of the changes in American academic life since the war, Christopher Jencks and David Riesman devoted a chapter to Catholic colleges. It ended with a pointed observation, "The important question...is not whether a few Catholic universities prove capable of competing with Harvard and Berkeley on the latter's terms, but whether Catholicism can provide an ideology or personnel for developing alternatives to the Harvard-Berkeley model of excellence."[19]

In some ways, the past 40 years have been a spirited conversation about this very topic, one that shows no sign of flagging. Doomsayers might see this conversation as evidence of uncertain identity, but I think it would be closer to the truth to say that it is a sign of good health. The comment supposedly uttered in exasperation, "A Catholic university is a university where everyone keeps asking, 'What is a Catholic university?'" points to a possibly quite meaningful truth at the heart of a sound theology of the Holy Spirit—like the Christian life, a Catholic university is a work in progress. And a lot of people feel they have a stake in the outcome and want to contribute their voices.

This 40-year conversation has produced an immense bibliography, including journals, dedicated websites, and similar resources and a huge number of initiatives in curriculum, student affairs, and campus ministry programming as well as many kinds of faculty and administrative staff formation programs. It has also produced some notable structural innovations. On almost any campus it is common now to have a mission or identity officer, a vice president or special assistant to the president, whose responsibilities include furthering the campus conversation about the Catholic dimensions of the institution's mission.

This 40-year conversation should encourage us to think that over time it

---

[19] Christopher Jencks and David Riesman, *The Academic Revolution* (New Brunswick, NJ: Transaction Publishers, 2001), p. 405.

will provide answers to our questions about student formation. My experience, however, tells me that the current steps on Catholic campuses toward strengthening student formation could have a clearer rationale and a more coherent strategy, that support for anything more elaborate is likely to be rather fragile in most institutions, and that a number of factors could still get in the way—the professional pressures on faculty and the de facto reward system they operate in, the scant knowledge many administrators and faculty have of theology and spirituality, the persuasion of students and their families that professional or preprofessional preparation is the main function of undergraduate education, the lure of online education and other technological solutions, and of course a lack of resources everywhere for implementing even effective programs. Under these very real pressures, students may be left to drift through their undergraduate years, being formed by happenstance, at best occasional consumers of such formational resources as are available to them—a retreat here, a service program there, perhaps a capstone course in senior year. Can we imagine an alternative, that students are encouraged to see that their college years have a shape and a direction, one that not only trains their minds and helps them mature socially but also has a spiritual dimension that can respond to their deepest longings for meaning and community, that there are maps for the journey, and that the adults in their lives—faculty, administrators, staff—agree about the main features of these maps and are eager to help them on their way? The remainder of this essay proposes a possible framework for thinking about student formation and some suggestions for implementing it.

A Framework for Thinking Strategically about Formation

Why did so many American colleges and universities, in Anthony Kronman's words, give up on the meaning of life? If Marsden is correct in thinking that the decisive factor was the alliance 19th-century liberal Protestantism made with the view that scholarly objectivity required the suspension of religious beliefs, then it is easy to understand why religion if it survived officially on campus, withdrew into divinity schools, departments of religious studies, and campus ministry programs, and why theology and the other disciplines would no longer talk to one another or share insights in their quests to understand the meaning of life or play roles, cooperative or even complementary, in the formation of students.

If we are to remedy this situation, I suggest we need a two-part framework.

One part will be an idea of the university that genuinely values empirical disciplines and professional models of training and the knowledges they produce but intentionally places these into conversation with religious accounts of human existence. The second part will be a picture of the psychological development of young adults as a work in progress that includes spiritual as well as intellectual and social dimensions and can be influenced by appropriate forms of pedagogy.

1. A Theologically Inclusive Idea of the University

"Whatever humanizes, divinizes." This is theologian Michael Himes's startling shorthand formula for expressing the Godward orientation of human existence and human activity. In talking about God, he says, we are talking about the absolute Mystery that lies at the root of all that exists. The "least wrong" way of imagining this God is as self-giving love, a love that acts out of no self-interest but simply from delight in giving. This self-giving love is the reason why anything exists. For Christians, it is perfectly expressed in human terms in one particular person, Jesus of Nazareth. If absolute Mystery has become human in him, says Himes, *is* human, then whatever makes us more human makes us more like God.[20]

Studying and teaching any discipline, therefore, is a holy activity because it teaches us to see what is *there*, what in the eyes of faith has been *given*. The continuing conversation about what is there, how it relates to being human, and what it means to be human can be thought of as the central purpose of the university, to which all the disciplines contribute in their own ways. So too all the resulting uses of knowledge, the immense edifice of human culture, the arts and sciences we have elaborated, the just social and political construction of our communities, can be seen as ways of enacting our humanity and, in the eyes of faith, of responding to divine self-giving.

A crucial corollary is that, in analogous but real ways, this perspective is available to those of different faiths or no religious faith at all. For, as John McDade argues, citing fellow theologian Bernard Lonergan, the instinct of faith is inseparable from the instinct for human progress, both instincts arising from the same root that God plants in our nature—the movement of the human heart toward a truth free from moral evil that threatens to dehumanize

---

[20] Michael Himes, "Living Conversation," in *Conversations on Jesuit Higher Education* (Fall 1995), pp. 23 and 26.

us and the desire to ground life in a purposeful framework so that, in the end, life matters and the efforts of human life are not lost in time or in death. Both instincts aspire to articulate and achieve a *shared, lasting human good*, a notion that is both internal to Christian faith experience, expressed in the Kingdom of God inaugurated by Jesus and his resurrection, and at the same time external to it, expressed in a vision of a just social community embodied in a range of cultures and accessible to everyone independent of their beliefs.[21] The mission of the Catholic university, I want to argue, is to create the conditions in which Christians, non-Christians, and post-Christians can engage in conversation about this shared, lasting human good and how to work together to bring it about.

When we try to specify the conditions for this conversation in a university setting, an interesting and ultimately productive paradox emerges. McDade points out that a genuine attempt to work from within the shared experience of Christians and unbelievers in a secular and critical culture has to be a meeting of equal partners in dialogue, built upon respect and friendship. But how can a believing Christian participating in this dialogue be silent about the decisive role that Jesus Christ has played in the Christian understanding of the world? For, if the incarnational perspective can be properly expressed by the statement, *The Word comes to dwell in human cultures and shape them*, it is also true that the teaching of Jesus and his death and resurrection entail a further statement, *The Word confronts and challenges human cultures by refusing to be assimilated by them.*

For McDade, the only adequate response to this question is that Christians cannot be silent about the Christian otherness of their experience and beliefs and what these have taught them because this is precisely the contribution they bring to the dialogue. He cites Rabbi Jonathan Sacks's view that contemporary secular culture, though it extends a tolerance to every religion, tends by the pressure of its liberal assumptions—skepticism about distinguishing between "right" and "wrong" beliefs, the privatization of belief, a tolerance of all perspectives as valid, the maximum freedom for individual choice, marginalization of faith from public life, and so forth—to modify each in a way that

---

[21] John McDade, "The Jesuit Mission and Dialogue with Culture" in *Jesuit Education 21: Conference Proceedings on the Future of Jesuit Higher Education*, edited by Martin R. Tripole (Philadelphia: St. Joseph's University Press, 2000), pp. 56–66. The passage McDade cites from Lonergan is from "Method in Theology," reprinted in *The Lonergan Reader*, edited by Elizabeth A. Morelli and Mark D. Morelli (Toronto, Ontario, CA: University of Toronto Press, second revised edition, 1977), p. 479.

removes from it every distinctive feature and weakens its internal sources of energy. Only internally strong and distinct moral communities, which maintain their sense of difference, Sacks argues, can act as the generative heart of cultural values and bring them to the public dialogue.

Contemporary college and university education, I suggest, offers an almost exact parallel to the situation Sacks is describing. That is why we need to create a space for an intentional presence of the Christian/Catholic voice in the university in order to have the kind of conversation that brings faith into productive engagement with other belief systems in the task of articulating and pursuing the shared, lasting human good. This conversation should be the distinctive intellectual characteristic of a Catholic college or university.

2. A Developmental Pedagogy

This will provide the second part of our formational framework. Recent decades have seen an enormous expansion of our understanding of the developmental journey of young adults, following the early work of Erik Erikson on adolescent identity and intimacy. William Perry has described the intellectual and ethical transitions of the college years. Arthur Chickering has worked out a detailed description of specific developmental vectors along which college students grow in intellectual and social competence. More recently, Jeffrey Arnett has proposed that the period of identity development and self-definition continues well beyond the college years, and that this period of *emerging adulthood*, roughly ages 18–28, constitutes a distinct developmental phase. A number of cultural factors, including changes in the labor force, the sexual revolution of the '60s, and new women's roles, have combined to delay marriage, commitment to a specific career, and financial independence—the traditional markers of adulthood. As a result, college and the following years form a period preoccupied with the same developmental issues. It is the age of *identity exploration*, of trying out various possibilities, especially in love and work. It is the age of *instability*. It is the most *self-focused* age of life. It is the age of *feeling in between*, in transition, neither adolescent nor adult. And it is the age of *possibilities*, when hopes flourish and young men and women have an unparalleled opportunity to transform their lives.[22]

What roles can we play, as faculty members and administrators, in helping student negotiate these transitions? I suggest, as a manageable hypothesis,

---

[22]   Jeffrey Jensen Arnett, *Emerging Adulthood* (New York: Oxford University Press, 2004), p. 8.

that development in the years of emerging adulthood can be understood as oc-
curring along three dimensions: intellectual, social, and spiritual.[23]

The *intellectual dimension* has to do with how young adults learn to balance context, observation, inherited truths, relationships, and growing critical
self-awareness in new ways of thinking and knowing. They discover that some
ways of composing truth and making moral choices are more adequate than
others, that some beliefs deserve allegiance because they are more persuasive and life-giving. Moving toward adulthood is seen as joining others in dis-
cerning what is adequate, worthy, and valuable. The *social dimension* is about
learning how to live with peers whose beliefs, values, sexual orientations, and
racial/ethnic/socioeconomic backgrounds may be different from their own;
how to negotiate the shift from inherited roles and relationships to a new
awareness of the person behind the masks for whom one now takes responsibility; and how to balance a new understanding of self and of the social communities to which one belongs. The *spiritual dimension* of development entails
critically reassessing the beliefs, practices, and tacit values of family and faith
community that sustained childhood and early adolescent religious identity
and appropriating them in forms more adequate to accumulated experience.
The religious challenge is in part intellectual but also more personal and intimate: how to locate oneself in a transcendent order of being or within a hori-
zon of ultimate significance that is trustworthy enough to ground a sense of
living fully and authentically; how to experience one's relationship to a God
whose image changes and becomes more complex.

This picture suggests several helpful ways of understanding development,
and therefore student formation, as a *process* that can be influenced: (1) These
are not three separate dimensions; they constantly interact with and influence
one another; and growth along one dimension often can't be understood without taking into account the other two dimensions. (2) Ideally, growth moves
toward integration as a student matures. This integration can be furthered by
design. (3) Orderly development is not inevitable. Students can resist it,
circumstances delay it, and—most important—teachers and other adults can
intentionally foster it by finding the right combination of challenge and support—challenge because students need to be helped to move away from com-

---

[23] These comments are worked out in more detail in a publication used at Boston College, *The
Journey into Adulthood: Understanding Student Formation*, published by the Intersections Project
(Boston College, 2006).

fortable ways of knowing and behaving, support because the new self that emerges is inevitably fragile and tentative.

A Deliberate Formational Strategy

How might we build on this framework to create a deliberate strategy to foster student formation? A helpful starting point is Michael Himes's suggestion that a college education can be thought of as a continuous conversation with multiple partners living and dead.[24] This is an appealing and not unfamiliar way of describing a liberal education, but what if we give it an intentional edge? At Boston College we have found it useful to work with the idea that all the adults in the university, whatever their role, can be thought of as expert conversation partners in the project of student formation.[25]

In this conversation we want students to move through a five-part dynamic, loosely drawn from Ignatian spirituality and the pedagogy of the early Jesuit schools: first, understand the context you're operating in; second, pay attention to your experience; third, reflect on its meaning; fourth, decide how to act; and fifth, evaluate the outcome.[26] The intention is that, by habituating students to practice and internalize this dynamic, they will appropriate it as their own and so lay the foundation for an adulthood where the practice of discernment about their experience and their actions becomes a way of life.

The remainder of this essay attempts to sketch out some ways a strategy of cultivating this expert conversation might operate in different areas of the university.

The Parallel Curriculum

I suggest we begin here because, though I suspect the parallel curriculum goes unnoticed by many who are skeptical about the whole idea of formation, it is a part of college life where formative intent and impact are striking once attention is drawn to it.

In his 2001 study of what works in college, *Making the Most of College:*

---

[24]   Himes, "Living Conversation," p. 27.

[25]   J. A. Appleyard, "An Experience of Ignatian Conversation," in *Human Development* 29:1 (Spring 2008), pp. 13–19.

[26]   *Ignatian Pedagogy: A Practical Approach* (Rome: General Curia of the Society of Jesus, 1993), reprinted in *The Jesuit Ratio Studiorum: 400th Anniversary Perspectives*, edited by V. J. Duminuco (New York, NY: Fordham University Press, 2000), pp. 248–263.

Students Speak Their Minds, Richard Light found that, when asked to think of a specific, critical incident or moment that had changed them profoundly, 80 percent of students chose a situation or event outside of the classroom.[27] I don't think this necessarily means that what happens outside the classroom is more important than what happens inside, but that for many or indeed most students nonacademic experiences may be the catalysts for significant learning, the places where the different dimensions of development fuse in a moment of insight or self-discovery.

Light's finding seems to be reflected in a phenomenon of campus life that I don't believe existed 30 or 40 years ago. A cluster of programs has come into existence that together constitute a whole new way of being a student. They amount to a parallel world, on the surface barely if at all connected to the curriculum, residential life, and the other structures we traditionally associate with a college education. These include extensive menus of religious retreats; service programs, local, national, and international, which require substantial commitments of time; immersion programs, international and domestic; and various weekend programs that address issues of college life or help students identify their gifts and the life directions these gifts imply.

The programs of this parallel curriculum differ from familiar extracurricular activities like the campus newspaper, the dramatic society, or student government in several ways. The most striking difference is that these programs, without exception, have a strongly explicit reflective component. Many have a minidevelopmental structure of their own: students begin as participants, then return as group leaders, and eventually take responsibility for running the programs. Participants invest a lot of time in them (one program at Boston College requires weekly meetings for seven months, two weekend retreats, and eight days of spring break). They develop a network of similarly involved friends, which may become the group they primarily identify with and socialize with. Students say they experience these programs as safe places where they can explore self and world and figure out the connections between their ideals, their social skills, and their classroom learning. They describe them as "life-changing" so often it has become a cliché. Most of the programs have an explicit faith dimension and a strong service ethos and most involve or culminate in an off-campus experience, as though organizers believe par-

27   Richard J. Light, *Making the Most of College: Students Speak Their Minds* (Cambridge, MA: Harvard University Press, 2001), p. 8.

ticipants have to get away from normal campus life in order to see things clearly. Finally, and most interestingly, they seem to have come into existence as deliberate interventions of administrators rather than because of any student demand, apparently out of a perception that something was missing in students' educational experience, that something needed to be remedied or enhanced.

It may be relevant—if I am correct in thinking that this parallel curriculum didn't exist 30 to 40 years ago—that its appearance was contemporaneous with the big leap in the academic reputation and institutional ambition of most Catholic colleges and universities. Did something happen then to make it harder to attend to students' rounded development as human beings in the classroom and residence halls? In any case, the parallel curriculum or whatever we want to call it has flourished on many campuses and become thoroughly inserted into the pattern of college life. I draw attention to it here for three reasons: It is an existing structure of programs aimed at fostering student development; it is a part of the institution's ecosystem under the control of the administration and therefore a prime resource for implementing an intentional student formation plan; and to the extent that administrators and especially faculty can be drawn into participating in its programs they quickly come to see the meaning and value of student formation.

The Core Curriculum

One would suppose from its name, and because, pragmatically, it is the part of the curriculum most amenable to influence by the administration, that the core would reflect the institutional mission. Unfortunately, most core programs lack a rationale more persuasive than the notion that some breadth of exposure to a variety of subject areas is good for you—some natural science, some humanities, some social science, and so forth, with Catholic colleges and universities adding some philosophy and some theology. As a result, students and their advisors often regard it as a burden to be gotten out of the way as soon as possible.

Could we imagine a core curriculum that embodied the two parts of the framework suggested here for a program of intentional student formation: a theological vision of the meaning of human life and a developmental organization of its requirements?

From a theological perspective, this curriculum would provide courses that explore the faith traditions that ground the belief systems of significant parts of humanity and how these have shaped the cultures of the world. It would provide courses that would support all students in exploring the content and contours of their own beliefs and more deeply appropriating those beliefs in their own lives. Moreover, a core curriculum grounded in a Christian incarnational view of reality would reflect several key implications of that view: that reason and rational analysis can enlighten our experience, that the forms of human culture—the sciences, arts, humanities, political and social structures, and so forth—are all necessary parts of our study as sources of understanding, and that the diverse forms of knowledge that result from academic exploration can illuminate one another and together move, however haltingly, toward convergence in an ever more comprehensive truth and wisdom that can guide our lives.

From a developmental perspective, the core should embody the image behind its name, and function as a central column or scaffolding on which the other parts of a student's education are supported and connected from freshman to senior year. Some institutions already have courses, usually optional, that introduce students to college as well as capstone courses that explore the issues of leaving college. Could we build on these initiatives and address developmental issues head-on, by providing in every one of the four years opportunities to reflect on the experience of college, in all its dimensions, intellectual, social, and spiritual, and explore the connections among the disciplines as well as their significance for the student's stance toward the world.

The proposed core curriculum at Boston College is an interesting example of this concept. A four-year framework envisions students' intellectual "exploration" being accompanied by a variety of courses and experiences fostering their "reflection" on how these explorations are related to their social and spiritual growth. An unusual feature of the proposal is that it envisions the development of this reflective component as the responsibility of academic personnel working with student affairs and mission and ministry personnel and it gives the ultimate oversight of the core as a whole to the vice presidents of these three areas.

The Major Curriculum

From a formational view, two broad generalizations about the part of the curriculum shaped by the departments and their majors come to mind. First, the curriculum of a particular major or academic discipline is by its nature a powerful structure for fostering a student's intellectual development, since any discipline will inevitably be organized in terms of introductory material and concepts, more advanced understanding and skills, and then relatively expert levels of competence and mastery. Second, typically, however, a department or discipline views its curriculum in terms of material to be covered and skills to be mastered rather than in terms of a pedagogy that deliberately exploits the developmental possibilities of this curriculum.

By the discipline's standards, a successful student is one who masters the content of the field and who can demonstrate the intellectual skills appropriate to it. But consider this curriculum from the undergraduate's perspective. He or she may find the first immersion exciting yet wrestle painfully with new concepts and the novel bewilderment of poor grades. There may be a long stretch of ups and downs and a vague sense of moving forward, or the student may experience moments of excitement when, say, an experience of service or an internship or an existential crisis suddenly throws a brilliant light on the significance of something covered in the classroom. Sometimes the student feels an escalating sense of self-possession and identity ("I'm getting good at this") or may not even recognize his or her own success and be mystified by a professor's praise. Or it may be that the student's whole sense of values is shaken by the course, leaving him or her struggling to recompose a new sense of self and world.

What if the curriculum in each discipline and the pedagogy employed were designed with the developmental trajectory and its challenges in mind, so that in addition to focusing on the subject matter and the skills appropriate to it, instructors would be conscious of maximizing the kind of reflection that moves development forward? Each discipline might be structured with introductory and intermediate courses leading to capstone experiences that pull together what students have learned and explore the significance of its unity. Moreover, what if students were challenged all along the way in exams and papers and reports not just to repeat back information and demonstrate skills but to think about such questions as: What am I understanding and failing to understand about this material? What does it imply? How is it connected to the other things I'm learning, in this discipline and in other areas? Where am I in growing into this discipline? What am I learning about the world and about myself?

Would a student move through such a curriculum with a greater sense of growing competence, self-awareness, understanding of the world, and perhaps vocational direction?

Centers and Institutes

Much like the parallel curriculum is what has been called "the hidden university"—the centers, think tanks, and institutes that seem to have come into existence because the ordinary functioning of the university doesn't quite serve the needs of administrators, faculty members, and even donors who want to focus attention on particular topics and problems or advance certain agendas. Most operate ad extra, that is, they want to influence public opinion or the thinking of scholarly peers beyond the campus. Less familiar are those focused ad intra, working to change the ordinary functioning of the university so that it is more likely to do something it doesn't ordinarily seem set up to do.

I can testify from personal experience about the effectiveness of one such program, created at Boston College in 2000 as a result of a grant from Lilly Endowment, one of many given to religiously affiliated institutions to encourage students to reflect on their vocations as Christians. We used the grant to create a number of programs to help students reflect on this dimension of their lives and, more broadly, since our students came from many religious backgrounds and none at all, on what the human vocation entails. We also realized that if the student programs were to succeed we would need to create programs to educate faculty and administrators about what we came to call student formation and to draw them into seeing how their own professional work might contribute crucially to this project.

These programs flourished, evolved, and continue to have an impact on the institutional culture. The most valuable outcome of the grant, however, may have been that it enabled us to gather from across the university a group of smart, experienced, and committed people to brainstorm about our project and to take part in a multiyear conversation about it that still continues. Some of these people became full-time staff and a much larger number eager friends of the project. Equally significant was that the project resulted in the creation of two permanent centers, the Intersections Program and the Center for Student Formation, which continue inventive programming and, more importantly, sustain a wide-ranging conversation across the campus about student formation.

Hiring and Forming Personnel

It would seem to be only common sense that if any institution doesn't recruit and hire personnel committed to its mission and capable of contributing to it, the mission will soon be in disarray. In the long view, this is probably the most important variable in the survival and flourishing of an institution's mission.

Disarray isn't exactly what happened in most Catholic colleges and universities in the heady days of expansion and upward movement in rankings during the middle and later decades of the 20th century, when the goal was to hire "the best person available," but something almost as counterproductive did: compartmentalization of responsibilities came to be taken as a given. An obvious example was the silent agreement that the faculty was responsible for the intellectual formation of students and other kinds of formation were someone else's responsibility, and the religious aspects of the institutional mission would be taken care of by the "religious professionals" on campus.

I don't think anyone in Catholic colleges and universities quite believes this anymore. The *desirability* of hiring faculty and staff sympathetic to the mission is widely acknowledged in principle. What this means, however, and how to go about it are much less clear. The mission may not be well articulated and can't be turned into agreed criteria for hiring. Those doing the hiring are often fainthearted about the concrete steps needed to introduce a consideration of mission into the process. For faculty, hiring processes are often wholly department based and impervious to any but token administrative input. Compartmentalization can appear necessary—this person suits this need, we'll look for mission fit the next time. I don't despair of vigorous efforts to hire for mission, but it is an uphill struggle.

A different—or in an ideal situation a complementary—approach is to create substantive faculty and staff formation programs around institutional mission, for example, week- or semester-long seminars on the institution's mission or summer institutes. Best of all would be a program spread across a colleague's working life involving varied types of experiences: seminars, religious retreats, service and immersion programs, the opportunity to take theology courses, pilgrimages to places associated with the charism of the founding religious congregation, and similar initiatives. Making these experiences available to faculty and staff is good. Even better would be to convey the sense that the institution genuinely values their participation, by providing time and stipends as appropriate, making clear that it considers these activities supportive of their professional development as part of the institution's mission, and rewards them accordingly.

Administrative Leadership

This is the topic of another paper in this collection so I shall mention only two obvious aspects of administrative leadership that bear on the project of student formation.

First, *leadership determines priorities and provides resources.* The mission and identity movement has flourished most where it has had strong administrative backing. If it is just one institutional concern among many ("assistant to the president for..."), it gets precisely that degree of attention and resources. Creating an intentional program of student formation will not be cheap. As George Marsden says about the more general project of building a first-rate Catholic university, "No such program to move in a direction counter to major historical trends is going to be accomplished with pocket change left over from normal university activities."[28]

Second, *leadership articulates the mission,* either personally or by seeing that this happens. Catholic colleges and universities have not always done this well. The vague terminology, secondhand slogans, and code language of so many mission statements suggest the institutions themselves have a poor understanding of what their being Catholic means. Articulating the mission and, specifically, the rationale and plan for a student formation project isn't just a matter of putting something on paper for the record. As philosopher Charles Taylor points out, moral goods exist only if we articulate them and the love of the articulated good moves us to good action.[29] Here, in a nutshell, is the rationale for clarifying the "difference" that a Catholic faith tradition makes to a college or university: love of this difference moves the various actors in the institution to pursue it.

Conclusion

A university and, in varying degrees, a college has multiple goals: to educate undergraduates, to pursue research, to train professionals, and to contribute to the community. I have been arguing that intentionally forming students, intellectually, socially, and spiritually, should be a central purpose of any

---

[28] George M. Marsden, "What Can Catholic Universities Learn from Protestant Examples?" in *The Challenge and Promise of a Catholic University*, edited by Theodore M. Hesburgh (Notre Dame, IN: University of Notre Dame Press, 1994), p. 197.

[29] Charles Taylor, *Sources of the Self: The Making of the Modern Identity* (Cambridge, MA: Harvard University Press, 1989), pp. 91–93.

undergraduate education. Catholic colleges and universities have historically understood this as part of their central mission and I don't know of any Catholic institution today that doesn't take seriously some degree of commitment to student formation. The question I have been trying to pose in this paper, though, is whether our formational efforts amount to more than separate points of light here and there on the campus, available to students who want to take advantage of them, unconnected by any coherent strategy, and therefore weakly effective in the face of powerful currents from a culture that prioritizes other goals for college education.

A remark of Howard Gray's, who helped design the programs Lilly funded at Boston College, has always seemed provocative to me: we need to turn events into programs and programs into structures. I would take this principle one step further: structures need to be grounded in a strategic vision. This paper proposes a two-part vision: a theological understanding of the university's mission and a developmental understanding of the student's educational journey and the role of faculty and staff in supporting that journey. I hope it will stimulate the kind of conversation this symposium hopes to encourage and the topic of student formation deserves.

"Catholic" as Descriptive of a University: A Canonical Perspective

ROBERT J. KASLYN, S.J.

DEAN OF THE SCHOOL OF CANON LAW, THE CATHOLIC UNIVERSITY OF AMERICA

C anon law does not replace Church teaching but serves it.[1] In 1965, Pope Paul VI said that "with changing conditions—with life evolving more rapidly—canon law is to be prudently reformed: namely, it must be accommodated to a new way of thinking [*novus habitus mentis*] proper to the Second Vatican Ecumenical Council, by which pastoral care and the new needs of the People of God are met." This "new way of thinking" required a new mind-set, a new approach to the law of the Church than that which had determined the formulation of the prior code.[2]

Changing the law, however, does not change its underlying theological presuppositions, foundation, or teaching. Pope John Paul II expressed this same fundamental principle in his apostolic constitution *Sacrae disciplinae leges,* promulgating the revised code in 1983 (apostolic constitutions are "considered the most solemn form of legal document issued by the Pope"[3]).

---

[1]   This paper will be using the *Codex Iuris Canonici Pii X Pontificis Maximi iussu digestus Benedicti Papae XV auctoritate promulgatus* (Rome: Typis Polyglottis Vaticanis, 1917) and the *Code of Canon Law, Latin-English Edition: New English Translation* (Washington, D.C.: CLSA, 2001).

[2]   Pope Paul VI, allocution, "*Ad E.mos Patres Cardinales et ad Consultores Pontificii Consilii Codici Iuris Canonici Recognoscendo,*" November 20, 1965, *Communicationes* 1 (1969), p. 41. The text of this allocution is also found in *Acta Apostolicae Sedis* 57 (1965), pp. 985–989.

[3]   Kurt Martens, "The Nature of Authority of Roman Documents," *Proceedings of the Sixty-Ninth Annual Convention of the CLSA* 69 (2007), p. 138.

The new code

> could be understood as a great effort to translate this same
> doctrine, that is, the conciliar ecclesiology, into canonical
> language. If, however, it is impossible to translate perfectly
> into canonical language the conciliar image of the Church,
> nevertheless, in this image there should always be found as
> far as possible its essential point of reference.[4]

This gives canon law a unique function in the Church, as Pope John Paul
stated in the same text:

> [T]he Code is in no way intended as a substitute for faith, grace
> and the charisms in the life of the Church and of the faithful. On
> the contrary, its purpose is rather to create such an order in the
> ecclesial society that, while assigning the primacy to faith, grace
> and the charisms, it at the same time renders easier their organic
> development in the life both of the ecclesial society and of the
> individual persons who belong to it.

This intimate nexus in the Church—in its nature of sacrament—between the
visible and the invisible, the human and the divine, prevents (or should pre-
vent) any false dichotomy between, for example, "The Church of Charity" and
"The Church of Law" or between "The Gospel" and "Law."[5]

Ecclesiological Perspective

In canons 208 to 223, the code includes a series of "obligations and rights"
of all the Christian faithful. Canon 209 requires that the faithful are always
obliged to maintain communion with the Church and "With great diligence
they are to fulfill the duties which they owe to the universal Church and the
particular church to which they belong according to the prescripts of the
law." Canon 223 asserts that the Christian faithful "must take into account

---

4   Pope John Paul II, *Sacrae disciplinae leges*, January 25, 1983.

5   See *Lumen Gentium* 8 in *Decrees of the Ecumenical Councils*, edited by Norman P. Tanner
(London: Sheed & Ward and Washington, D.C.: Georgetown University Press, 1990),
vol. 2, p. 854.

the common good of the Church, the rights of others, and their own duties toward others." These two canons offer canonical expression of *Lumen Gentium* 9: "It has pleased God, however, to sanctify and save men and women not individually and without regard for what binds them together but to set them up as a people who would acknowledge him in truth and serve him in holiness."[6]

As one consequence, the communal dimension of faith is fundamental to any ecclesiology and hence to the place and role of canon law. This communal dimension is expressed through, for example, the obligation to maintain communion incumbent upon Catholics; the fact that rights and obligations are not a personal prerogative but rather a communal exercise; the necessity to consider the common good when acting.

The obligation to maintain communion with the Church obligates both individuals and institutions: persons physical and juridical.[7] Through valid baptism, a person becomes a person in the Church with rights and obligations (see canons 96 and 204); nonphysical persons may become subject of rights and obligations either by the law itself or decree of competent authority (see canon 114) and thereby become juridic persons, the subjects of rights and obligations (see canon 113 §1).

At its most basic expression, those in full communion with the Church are those joined with Christ in the Church's visible structure through the bonds of the profession of faith, the sacraments, and ecclesiastical governance (see canon 205). "Full communion" includes a broad spectrum of ongoing relationships between an individual and the Church. It is a dynamic, not a static concept, but one with a fundamental content indicated by the bonds of faith, sacraments, and governance. Stating that one is in full communion with

---

[6] *Decrees of the Ecumenical Councils*, vol. 2, p. 855. On the concept of *communio* ecclesiology, see John Beal, "From the Heart of the Church to the Heart of the World: Ownership, Control, and Catholic Identity of Institutional Apostolates in the United States," in *Sponsorship in the United States Context: Theory and Praxis*, edited by Rosemary Smith, S.C., Warren Brown, O.M.I., and Nancy Reynolds, S.P. (Washington, D.C.: Canon Law Society of America, 2006), pp. 31–48.

[7] See canon 113 §1: "In the Church, besides physical persons, there are also juridic persons, that is, subjects in canon law of obligations and rights which correspond to their nature." Through valid baptism, a person becomes a person in the Church with rights and obligations (see cc. 96 and 204); nonphysical persons may become subject of rights and obligations either by the law itself or decree of competent authority (see c. 114 §1) and thereby become, analogously and as juridic persons, the subjects of rights and obligations. For a treatment of juridic personality and Catholic universities, see William King, "Sponsorship by Juridic Persons," in *Sponsorship in the United States Context: Theory and Praxis*, pp. 49–72.

the Church imposes certain fundamental obligations upon the individual. "Full communion" is not simply determined by the individual's own ideas of that which is constitutive of full communion.

My fundamental argument is that the very desire to continue to describe itself as Catholic creates a theological obligation as strong as, if not stronger, than any juridic relationship. Such an obligation arises inasmuch as that desire necessarily reflects an active response to the Church's self-identity and self-understanding as expressed in the conciliar decree on ecumenism, *Unitatis redintegratio* 3:

> For it is only through Christ's Catholic Church, which is the all-embracing means of salvation, that the fullness of the means of salvation can be attained. We believe that Our Lord entrusted all the blessings of the New Covenant to the one apostolic college, of which Peter is the head, in order to establish the one Body of Christ on earth into which all should be fully incorporated who belong in any way to the people of God.[8]

Any undertaking that considers itself Catholic must accept this ecclesiological perspective or risk being considered or judged self-contradictory in its very identity.[9]

From a canonical perspective, each institution that describes itself as Catholic will possess a juridic status that reflects its identity. "Juridic status" does not have one precise meaning that pertains to each and every institution, but varies according to the canonical status of the particular institution. Each juridic relationship is unique—in its specific relationship with competent Church authority; in its statutes; in its authority structures, membership, and purpose. The specific parameters of a university's juridic personality must be assessed from the perspective of its founding documents; norms, by-laws, statutes; archival documentation; and civil incorporation.

A recognized religious institute in the Church possesses public juridic

---

[8] Decrees of the *Ecumenical Councils*, vol. 2, pp. 910–911.

[9] The real possibility of religious indifferentism arises in reference to *Unitatis redintegratio* and *Lumen Gentium*, in particular with those Catholics who reject (or those who, at the least, choose not to accept publicly or to present) the Church's self-understanding in order to be more accepting of other religious denominations and faiths. But as is clear from ecumenical dialogue, one does not encourage or foster dialogue by denying one's own identity.

personality and has the right to acquire, possess, administer, and alienate temporal goods (see canon 634, §1). To the extent that the religious institute "acquired" and/or "possessed" a particular institution, to that extent that institution participated in the public juridic personality of the institute. The only way to sever that relationship is through canonical alienation and not simply through civil alienation. The common presumption that civil incorporation and the concomitant establishment of a lay board of trustees severs a preexisting juridic relationship between a Catholic university and the Catholic Church cannot, in my judgment, stand very close scrutiny. A preexisting canonical status can only be changed through canonical means.

"The McGrath thesis," named after John McGrath, maintains (according to John Beal's summary) that "when institutional apostolates are civilly incorporated, they acquire identities separate, both civilly and canonically, from those of their religious sponsors. Therefore, the property of these sponsored apostolates is no longer 'church property' subject to the regulatory norms of canon law and these institutions themselves are governed solely by the norms of civil law, except to the extent that their state-recognized charters and by-laws incorporate a role for the religious sponsor in governance."[10] "The Maida thesis," named after Adam Maida (later cardinal), holds in contrast that "civil incorporation does not per se alter the canonical status of institutional apostolates and their property."[11] The responsibility lies upon the institution to rectify the situation canonically.

Two further points are essential in this context. First, when a Catholic university has possessed public juridic personality through its founding religious institute, canonical implementation of civil incorporation must decide if the institution will henceforth possess juridic personality and if this personality will be public or private; the authority competent to recognize such status and to review or approve the statutes, etc. Public juridic persons are "closely governed by ecclesiastical authority" whereas private juridic persons enjoy more autonomy and are governed by their own statutes.[12] Not every institution

---

[10]   Beal, p. 37. See John McGrath, *Catholic Institutions in the United States: Canonical and Civil Law Status* (Washington, D.C.: The Catholic University of America Press, 1968).

[11]   Adam Maida, *Ownership, Control and Sponsorship of Catholic Institutions: A Practical Guide* (Harrisburg, PA: Pennsylvania Catholic Conference, 1975).

[12]   See Robert T. Kennedy, "Juridic Persons (cc. 11–121)" in *New Commentary on the Code of Canon Law*, edited by John P. Beal, et al. (New York/Mahwah, NJ: Paulist Press, 2000), p. 161.

of higher education will—or should—possess the same juridic status.

Second, if an institution accepts the McGrath thesis, at least as effective civilly, the difficult question of the subject of alienation remains; in admittedly simplistic terms, "What was alienated civilly?" Does alienation refer only to property and governance? Or did the institution intend, directly or indirectly, to alienate its usage of the description Catholic? The answer depends on a case-by-case analysis; I raise the issue inasmuch as the argument could be made that civil alienation of property and governance also possesses implications for a given institution's continued use of the word Catholic as descriptive of itself. The alienation issue raises numerous questions: To what extent does such transfer include or exclude responsibility to maintain the Catholic identity of the institution? To what extent does the founding religious institute or diocese have a legitimate "interest" in the institution? Is it, for example, recognized as a "major donor" of the institution with certain rights as such?

Most fundamentally, however, the question of Catholic identity must enter into the decision. At times, administrators presume a "juridic relationship" is based solely on personhood (human or juridic), whereas a broader concept of a juridic relationship, in fact, results from the obligation and the desire to maintain communion with the Church and therefore describe oneself as Catholic. An institution, even one without juridic personality (private or public), retains the obligation to maintain communion with the Church if it wishes to describe itself as Catholic and wishes to maintain its ties with the founding religious institute.

Difficulties arise when an institution has carefully and clearly followed civil law regulations concerning governance but has ignored or given second place to canonical norms. Until a particular institution clarifies its canonical status, its relationship with the Church (understood in the broad sense as including the Christian faithful as well as specific authorities such as the diocesan bishop) will remain fraught with minefields. To reiterate: neither "canonical status" nor "juridic relationship" are univocal concepts; both indicate a broad spectrum of relationships between a particular institution and competent Church authority. A juridic relationship exists inasmuch as an institution calls itself Catholic but the details of that relationship need specification for each situation.

As I said above, the Catholic university's theological obligation arises from its active response to the Church's self-identity and self-understanding as "the all-embracing means of salvation." The role and place of ecclesiology necessarily raises the issue of the magisterium of the Church. The dogmatic constitution on divine revelation, *Dei Verbum*, teaches "The task of authentically interpreting the word of God, whether in its written form or in that of tradition, has been entrusted only to those charged with the church's ongoing teaching function (*soli vivo ecclesiae magisterio concreditum est*), whose authority is exercised in the name of Jesus Christ."[13]

I will return to the role of the magisterium in the relationship between the Catholic university and the Church below. The fundamental principle, however articulated in particular circumstances, is that the "single sacred deposit of the word of God, entrusted to the Church"—Scripture and Tradition—and the magisterium are integral to one another and must be taken into consideration by theologians, including those who teach in departments of theology in Catholic universities. As Avery Dulles describes the relationship in *The Craft of Theology*,

> Both theology and the ecclesiastical magisterium must operate
> in the context of the whole Church as the primary recipient and
> bearer of divine revelation. The diversity of functions, since it
> exists only within the prior unity of the People of God, cannot
> be understood as separation or antagonism. Within the Church,
> theologians and hierarchical teachers depend in many ways
> upon one another.[14]

Describing an undertaking as "Catholic in inspiration," or "in the Catholic tradition" or perhaps more exasperatingly "in the tradition of" a given religious institute (as though the institute qua institute could or would exist independently of its juridic relationship with the Catholic Church) may simply be an attempt to avoid the responsibilities associated with using the name Catholic. The magisterium of the Church has a particular function to exercise; maintaining communion with the Church cannot be separated from maintaining communion with the magisterium of the Church.

This statement requires much greater elaboration than is possible here. Suffice it to say, the code in canons 749 to 755 recognizes a variety of levels of Church teaching—not all magisterial teaching is of the same weight. But

---

[13]   *Dei Verbum* 10, in *Decrees of the Ecumenical Councils*, vol. 2, p. 975.

[14]   Avery Cardinal Dulles, *The Craft of Theology* (New York: Crossroad, 1992), p. 107.

before these nuances can be used in interpretation, a fundamental acceptance of the Church's magisterium is required. An institution that calls itself Catholic must be open to other faiths but not to the extent or at the cost of denying its own Catholicity. Use of the term Catholic is necessarily exclusive— or else a denial of fundamental truths of the faith.

Donum Veritatis: On the Ecclesial Vocation of the Theologian, issued by the Congregation for the Doctrine of the Faith in 1990, offers an ideal: "The living Magisterium of the Church and theology, while having different gifts and functions, ultimately have the same goal: preserving the People of God in the truth which sets free and thereby making them 'a light to the nations.' This service to the ecclesial community brings the theologian and the Magisterium into a reciprocal relationship."[15] The instruction recognizes the essential role both play:

> the theologian has the duty to make known to the Magisterial authorities the problems raised by the teaching in itself, in the arguments proposed to justify it, or even in the manner in which it is presented. He should do this in an evangelical spirit and with a profound desire to resolve the difficulties. His objections could then contribute to real progress and provide a stimulus to the Magisterium to propose the teaching of the Church in greater depth and with a clearer presentation of the arguments.[16]

Obviously, a careful balancing act is required, on the part both of theologians and on the part of the magisterium. This explains the need to clarify the "juridic relationship" of the institution.

Donum Veritatis recognizes the theologian's necessary role of raising questions about a specific teaching or its presentation. But the Catholic theologian, while recognizing the reality of theological pluralism in the Church as well as outside it, must also recognize that as a Catholic certain teachings must be accepted with "divine and catholic faith" (see canon 750, §1). Such is necessary for the theologian not only to remain Catholic but to remain in communion with the community of faith. The specific role of the institution

---

[15] Congregation for the Doctrine of the Faith, *Donum Veritatis: On the Ecclesial Vocation of the Theologian* (Vatican City: Libreria Editrice Vaticana, 1990), #21.

[16] Ibid., #30.

in reference to those who teach theology must reflect its juridic status.

Legal Texts Influencing the Relationship between the Catholic University and the Catholic Church

One canon is essential to the relationship between Catholic universities and canon law and this primarily from the perspective of the university and its fundamental self-understanding. Canon 808 states: "Even if it is in fact Catholic, no university is to bear the title or name of Catholic university without the consent of competent ecclesiastical authority." (While the canon pertains only to universities established after November 27, 1983, the fundamental perspective upon which it is based is essential: a particular institution wishes to describe itself as Catholic.)

The fundamental issue is not the subsidiary one of who may or may not use the word "Catholic" in describing their service or who may allow use of the term, but rather the public perception of that service. Use of the word Catholic indicates that a given association or organization is in communion with the Church and with its fundamental teaching and principles and therefore is different from an organization that exists independently of any faith community or church, including the Catholic Church. Succinctly, using the word Catholic must mean something essential to the purposes of that group and hence the group, undertaking, or university requests use of the word Catholic. Interestingly enough, requesting use of the word "Catholic" as descriptive of its purpose and teleology would, according to the conciliar decree, apply uniquely to apostolates begun by the lay faithful (see *Apostolicam Actuositatem* 24).

While the competent ecclesiastical authority may consent to the use of the name Catholic, the undertaking must first request the use of the word to describe itself. Using the name "Catholic" is not simply a static description but rather indicates a dynamic reality; use of the adjective or noun Catholic indicates that the undertaking is in communion with the Church. Describing Catholics as "living in full communion" admits of varying degrees; this is one aspect of the human condition. Minimally, the bond of faith means acceptance of the creed but to the extent that an individual or institution wishes to maintain his, her, or its Catholicity, to that extent the individual or institution must accept what is integral to the deposit of faith.

This dynamic nature is constitutive of *communio* and thus of *communio* ecclesiology, and consequently of maintaining communion with the Church:

the fundamental state of a Catholic person (physical or juridic) is "being communion," that is, an existential state that ultimately derives from God's self-communication to an individual and the concomitant necessity of a response to this self-communication. (The phrase "being communion" derives from the *instrumentum laboris* of the 1994 Synod of Bishops: "First and foremost the accent must be placed on 'being' communion, and afterward on 'doing' something. Action cannot precede being."[17])

Understood in this way, "being communion" (as graced event) is the presupposition grounding or allowing a particular person (physical or juridic) to "be in communion with the Church." As much as maintaining communion with the Church is itself a dynamic concept, so too, the undertaking calling itself Catholic must dynamically maintain communion with the Church. Individuals must respond to the offer of grace and live their lives in communion with the Church; juridic persons, by describing themselves as Catholic (for example, in a mission statement or other fundamental documents or through its establishment), similarly choose to maintain communion with the Church inasmuch as the individuals representing a juridic person express their desire to participate in the mission of the Church by describing themselves as Catholic. I would argue that for this reason even an institution that has used the word "Catholic" in the past and wishes to continue to use the word is obliged to maintain communion with the Catholic Church.

This obligation to maintain communion with the Church begins with the statement that a given Catholic university considers itself Catholic. This obligation prescinds from the question of whether the institution possesses juridic personality in the Catholic Church or not. In other words, the desire (and the will) to implement norms of the Church by the university must arise, first, from the desire to be considered as Catholic, by itself and by others. Where a juridic relationship does exist—through its establishment or a decree of competent authority—the obligation to maintain communion obtains greater force inasmuch as it is a faith commitment and a legal commitment.

Universities wishing to exist in communion with the Catholic Church will utilize certain texts (which I will examine) to assist them in maintaining communion with the Church. These texts present necessary principles to those who comprise the university that chooses to describe itself as Catholic.

---

[17] Vatican Synod Secretariat, "The Consecrated Life and Its Role in the Church and in the World: Working Paper for October 1994 World Synod of Bishops," *Origins* 24 (June 30, 1994), p. 118.

The Code of Canon Law

First, as already noted, the basic legal text for the (Latin) Catholic Church is the *Code of Canon Law*. To understand the canons pertaining to Catholic universities, one must appreciate the context in which these canons are situated, namely, in Book III, "The Teaching Munus" (function, responsibility, office), which articulates the basic principles of the teaching or prophetic *munus* of the Church. (The prior code contained similar canons under the title "The Ecclesiastical Magisterium.") Book III begins with canon 747:

§ 1. The Church, to which Christ the Lord has entrusted the deposit of faith so that with the assistance of the Holy Spirit it might protect the revealed truth reverently, examine it more closely, and proclaim and expound it faithfully, has the duty and innate right, independent of any human power whatsoever, to preach the gospel to all peoples, also using the means of social communication proper to it.

§ 2. It belongs to the Church always and everywhere to announce moral principles, even about the social order, and to render judgment concerning any human affairs insofar as the fundamental rights of the human person or the salvation of souls requires it.

The deposit of faith has been entrusted to the Church in order to protect, examine, proclaim, and expound it under the guidance of the Spirit. *Lumen Gentium* 12 states:

"The holy people of God has a share, too, in the prophetic role [*munere*] of Christ [...].The universal body of the faithful, who have received the anointing of the holy one (see 1 Jn 2, 20, and 27), cannot be mistaken in belief....Through this sense of faith which is aroused and sustained by the Spirit of truth, the people of God, under the guidance of the sacred magisterium to which it is faithfully obedient, receives no longer the words of human beings but truly the word of God."[18]

---

[18] *Decrees of the Ecumenical Councils*, vol. 2, p. 858.

Both dimensions of the one reality must be kept in balance: the inerrancy in belief of all the faithful in matters of faith and morals and the specific *munus* of the college of bishops (including the Roman pontiff) as constituting the authoritative magisterium. As already noted in reference to *Dei Verbum*, the magisterium has a constitutive role to fulfill in the Church; such a constitutive role does not deny the necessity of theologians researching, publishing, and interacting with the magisterium while maintaining communion with the Church.

Any understanding of a Catholic university must recognize and accept that it cannot separate itself from the context of participating in the mission of the Church: the entire Church is entrusted with the deposit of faith; the entire Church is at its service. Catholic universities therefore constitute a significant means to fulfill the task entrusted to the Church: to proclaim the good news of Jesus Christ. A university that considers itself in any way Catholic is an institution that fosters the mission of the Church, whether it uses the name Catholic or not.

The institution necessarily participates in the teaching or prophetic *munus* and therefore must fulfill the fundamental obligations to maintain communion and to foster the common good. Academia and the Church can and must coexist for each to fulfill its proper mission. "[S]ince theology is a branch of knowledge, it ought to have a place in a university, since a university is a place in which universal knowledge is taught," Avery Dulles states in a discussion of John Henry Newman's defense of theology as a university discipline:

> When religion or even revealed religion is excluded, the other branches of knowledge tend to fill the vacuum. [...] In so doing, these other disciplines exceed their proper competence. Thus the university suffers not only from the absence of a branch of knowledge that ought to be there, but from the distortion of other branches that seek to compensate for that absence.[19]

In a university that considers itself Catholic, its academic credentials and rigor are reinforced through the study of theology, and particularly, Catholic theology.

---

[19] Dulles, *The Craft of Theology*, p. 153.

Ex Corde Ecclesiae

Ex Corde Ecclesiae, "from the heart of the Church," is an apostolic constitution promulgated by Pope John Paul II on August 15, 1990.[20] The pope begins (quoting an earlier address) by describing the function of a university: "A Catholic University's privileged task is 'to unite existentially by intellectual effort two orders of reality that too frequently tend to be placed in opposition as though they were antithetical: the search for truth, and the certainty of already knowing the fount of truth.'"[21]

Revelation itself reflects the fundamental unity of faith (the fount of truth) and reason (the search for truth). This again demonstrates the incarnational (or theandric) nature of the Church: a description of the Church cannot choose between a visible assembly or a spiritual community, between an earthly society or the Mystical Body of Christ, precisely because inasmuch as Jesus Christ is both divine *and* human, the Church in analogy with the Incarnation is both a visible assembly *and* a spiritual community, an earthly society *and* the Mystical Body of Christ. The reality is not faith or reason but faith *and* reason; not academic freedom or Church magisterium but academic freedom *and* Church magisterium; not Catholicity or academic rigor but Catholicity *and* academic rigor.

Historical development, however, has led to the creation of an apparent dichotomy between them. That false separation between faith and reason also contributed to the apparent separation, ultimately false, between the university and the Church, between academics and the magisterium. As already noted, maintaining communion with the Church is a dynamic, not static, reality. John Paul proceeds from this dynamism in stating:

> Catholic Universities are called to a continuous renewal, both as "Universities" and as "Catholic." For, "What is at stake is the *very meaning of scientific and technological research, of social life and of culture,* but, on an even more profound level, what is at stake is *the very meaning of the human person.*" Such renewal requires a clear awareness that, by its Catholic character, a University is made

---

[20] For the text of *Ex Corde Ecclesiae*, see www.vatican.va/holy_father/john_paul_ii/ apost_constitutions/documents/hf_jp-ii_apc_15081990_ex-corde-ecclesiae_en.html (accessed June 12, 2013).

[21] *Ex Corde Ecclesiae* 1.

> more capable of conducting an *impartial* search for truth,
> a search that is neither subordinated to nor conditioned by
> particular interests of any kind (emphasis his).[22]

On the practical level, how does a university invite both aspects: skepticism and the Catholic faith tradition? For Pope Benedict, in his Regensburg address, the Catholic faith tradition of the university so grounds the academic enterprise that skepticism is addressed, and overcome, directly by academic means. The university that wishes to consider itself Catholic can simultaneously demand academic rigor and reflect communion with the Church in its policies; in its public face (that is, the perception of the university's religious identity by those not directly affiliated with it); and in its articulation of Catholic teaching on particular points integral to contemporary culture.[23]

As Pope John Paul writes in *Ex Corde Ecclesiae*, "besides the teaching, research and services common to all Universities, a Catholic University, by *institutional commitment,* brings to its task the inspiration and light of the *Christian message.*" Therefore, for the Catholic university,

> Catholic ideals, attitudes and principles penetrate and inform
> university activities in accordance with the proper nature and au-
> tonomy of these activities. In a word, being both a University and
> Catholic, it must be both a community of scholars representing
> various branches of human knowledge, and an academic institu-
> tion in which Catholicism is vitally present and operative.[24]

A university that wishes to describe its role in the world as both academically rigorous and in fidelity to the Catholic Church can do so, despite attempts to separate academic rigor from academic research, or faith from reason. As Pope Benedict noted in reference to the University of Regensburg, where he had taught, radical skepticism about the absence of any need for a

---

[22] *Ex Corde Ecclesiae* 7.

[23.] See Pope Benedict XVI lecture, "Faith Reason, and the University. Memories and Reflections." September 12, 2006, available on the website of the Holy See: http://www.vatican.va/holy_father/benedict_xvi/speeches/2006/september/documents/hf_ben-xvi_spe_20060912_university-regensburg_en.html (accessed June 11, 2013).

[24] Ibid., 14; Pope John Paul cites *L'Université Catholique dans le monde moderne. Document final du 2ème Congrès des Délégués des Universités Catholiques,* § 1 as the source for these characteristics.

faculty of theology given that God does not exist could and did coexist within an academic community that has made a commitment to the Catholic faith. The university, however, must be unequivocal in its commitment to being Catholic, to being in communion; it cannot emphasize nonexclusivity or in-clusiveness to the point that its very identity as Catholic is threatened, or, perhaps worse, not even publicly recognized.

Application of *Ex Corde Ecclesiae* in the United States

The third important document is the American bishops' "Application of *Ex Corde Ecclesiae* in the United States, approved by the bishops in November 1999 and granted recognition by the Congregation for Bishops in May 2000."[25] *Ex Corde Ecclesiae* requires that its "General Norms...be applied concretely at the local and regional levels by Episcopal Conferences and other Assemblies of Catholic Hierarchy in conformity with the *Code of Canon Law* and complementary Church legislation, taking into account the Statutes of each University or Institute and, as far as possible and appropriate, civil law."[26]

Recognizing the importance of the Church understood as communion, the bishops explain that "The richness of communion illuminates the ecclesial relationship that unites the distinct, and yet complementary, teaching roles of bishops and Catholic universities." In this communion,

> the teaching responsibilities of the hierarchy and of the Catholic universities retain their distinctive autonomous nature and goal but are joined as complementary activities contributing to the fulfillment of the Church's universal teaching mission. The com-munion of the Church embraces both the pastoral work of bish-ops and the academic work of Catholic universities, thus linking the bishops' right and obligation to communicate and safeguard the integrity of Church doctrine with the right and obligation of Catholic universities to investigate, analyze and communicate all truth freely.[27]

---

[25] One source for this text is the web page of the United States Conference of Catholic Bishops, http://nccbuscc.org/bishops/application_of_excordeecclesiae.shtml (accessed June 1, 2013).

[26] General Norms, Article 1 §2.

[27] *Ex Corde Ecclesiae* 2.

Here *communio* does not refer to an amorphous, inchoate relationship between a given institution and the Church nor, in the words of the *Nota Praevia* to *Lumen Gentium*, to "some kind of vague disposition, but [to] an organic reality which requires a juridical form and is animated by charity."[28]

As one consequence, and while recognizing the responsibility of a Catholic university to academic rigor in cooperation with the wider academic community, both nationally and universally, "The Application of *Ex Corde Ecclesiae*" encourages mutual trust between the institution and the ecclesiological authorities founded upon frequent and open communication (#4) as well as close and consistent cooperation between them both (#5) and continuing dialogue between the two (#6). On the practical level, it offers the following guidelines for institutions that wish to describe themselves as Catholic. They must: "set out clearly in their official documentation their Catholic character and...implement in practical terms their commitment to the essential elements of Catholic identity." Doing so includes:

1. Commitment to be faithful to the teachings of the Catholic Church;

2. Commitment to Catholic ideals, principles and attitudes in carrying out research, teaching and all other university activities, including activities of officially recognized student and faculty organizations and associations, and with due regard for academic freedom and the conscience of every individual;

3. Commitment to serve others, particularly the poor, underprivileged and vulnerable members of society;

4. Commitment of witness of the Catholic faith by Catholic administrators and teachers, especially those teaching the theological disciplines, and acknowledgment and respect on the part of non-Catholic teachers and administrators of the university's Catholic identity and mission;

5. Commitment to provide courses for students on Catholic moral and religious principles and their application to critical areas such as human life and other issues of social justice;

6. Commitment to care pastorally for the students, faculty, administration and staff;

---

[28] See *Lumen Gentium, Nota Explicativa Praevia* 2, in *Decrees of the Ecumenical Councils*, vol. 2, p. 899.

7. Commitment to provide personal services (health care, counseling and guidance) to students, as well as administration and faculty, in conformity with the Church's ethical and religious teaching and directives; and

8. Commitment to create a campus culture and environment that is expressive and supportive of a Catholic way of life.[29]

The rationale for implementing these and similar policies and practices is ultimately the choice of the university to describe itself as Catholic and in communion with the Church. A juridic relationship—if such exists and dependent upon its proper norms approved by competent authority—strengthens the necessity of implementing such policies and practices. Nonetheless, the fundamental obligation arises from the need to maintain communion with the Church in order to describe itself as Catholic.

Two issues often arise in discussion of the university's identity: the question of hiring Catholic faculty and that of the theology faculty's relation of Catholic teaching. About the first, "The Application *of Ex Corde Ecclesiae*" states in 4a:

> In accordance with its procedures for the hiring and retention of professionally qualified faculty and relevant provisions of applicable federal and state law, regulations and procedures, the university should strive to recruit and appoint Catholics as professors so that, to the extent possible, those committed to the witness of the faith will constitute a majority of the faculty. All professors are expected to be aware of and committed to the Catholic mission and identity of their institutions.

The question that confronts a university that considers itself Catholic is the extent to which its Catholic identity can be maintained, fostered, and manifested without significant numbers of Catholics on the faculty. A Catholic association needs Catholic members in order to ensure its Catholicity. It can

---

[29] These are actually numbers 5 through 12 in "Application," following the "four distinctive characteristics that are essential for Catholic identity," which are: "(1) Christian inspiration in individuals and the university community; (2) Reflection and research on human knowledge in the light of the Catholic faith; (3) Fidelity to the Christian message in conformity with the magisterium of the Church; (4) Institutional commitment to the service of others."

hire non-Catholics but must insist on their recognition and acceptance that the institution considers itself Catholic and therefore in their manner of acting must express agreement with that Catholic identity. Hiring faculty who are inimical to Catholicism or to Catholic tradition is simply a contradiction in terms.

In reference to the second issue, "The Application *of Ex Corde Ecclesiae"* states:

> Both the university and the bishops, aware of the contributions made by theologians to Church and academy, have a right to expect them to present authentic Catholic teaching. Catholic professors of the theological disciplines have a corresponding duty to be faithful to the Church's magisterium as the authoritative interpreter of Sacred Scripture and Sacred Tradition.

The issue here is the Catholic identity of the institution, not the question of academic freedom. The canard that Catholic faith limits academic freedom is belied by the Catholic academic tradition. As Avery Dulles has noted, "It would be sheer ignorance to deny the quality of scholarship that emanates from some of the major Catholic universities and theological faculties in the United States and in many other countries. To define university education so as to exclude such institutions and faculties is evidence of a parochialism that is, in its own way, sectarian."[30]

Further, academic freedom is itself an inchoate term with varying meanings, Dulles notes, but then argues that "Every theologian should enjoy academic freedom, in the sense of a right to inquire, publish and teach according to the norms of the discipline. But because theology is an essentially ecclesial discipline, the freedom of the theologian must not be absolutized over and against other elements in the community of faith." He continues:

> While the freedom of the professor as an individual scholar should be respected, it should be seen in the context of other values. One such value is the integrity of Catholic theology as a meditation on the shared faith of the whole Church. [...] Another such value is the maintenance of sound doctrine, even in

---

[30]   Dulles, *The Craft of Theology*, p. 172.

> matters that are not strictly of faith. [...] the rights of the theologian as an academician become real only when situated in this ecclesial framework.[31]

A university that describes itself as Catholic must necessarily contextualize itself with an ecclesial framework or else its academic life is self-contradictory to its identity.

The *Mandatum*

"The Application *of Ex Corde Ecclesiae*" requires that "Catholics who teach the theological disciplines in a Catholic university...have a *mandatum* granted by competent ecclesiastical authority."[32] It concerns the relationship between an individual professor and competent ecclesiastical authority and not—or not necessarily the Catholic university itself, which can require its theologians to have the *mandatum* but is not required to. The professor, not the university, is obligated to seek the *mandatum*, although (referring to canon 810, §1) if a professor without it "continues to teach a theological discipline, the university must determine what further action may be taken in accordance with its own mission and statutes."[33]

The *mandatum* is "fundamentally an acknowledgment by Church authority that a Catholic professor of a theological discipline is a teacher within the full communion of the Catholic Church." It does not imply "an appointment, authorization, delegation or approbation of one's teaching by Church authorities. Those who have received a *mandatum* teach in their own name in virtue of their baptism and their academic and professional competence, not in the name of the Bishop or of the Church's magisterium. The *mandatum* recognizes the professor's commitment and responsibility to teach authentic Catholic doctrine and to refrain from putting forth as Catholic teaching anything contrary to the Church's magisterium." It expresses "a necessary though complementary service to the Church that requires ongoing and mutually respectful dialogue" between bishops and theologians.

---

[31] Ibid., pp. 175–176.

[32] Footnote 40 to the text cites canon 812 and *Ex Corde Ecclesiae*, II, Art. 4, §3 in reference to this requirement.

[33] "The Application of *Ex Corde Ecclesiae*," footnote 41.

"The Application *of Ex Corde Ecclesiae*" gives a procedure for receiving the *mandatum* (this is a summary of the main points):

1. The competent ecclesiastical authority to grant the *mandatum* is the bishop of the diocese in which the Catholic university is located; he may grant the *mandatum* personally or through a delegate.

2. Without prejudice to the rights of the local bishop, a *mandatum*, once granted, remains in effect wherever and as long as the professor teaches unless and until withdrawn by competent ecclesiastical authority.

3. The *mandatum* should be given in writing. The reasons for denying or removing a *mandatum* should also be in writing.[34]

It notes, "The attestation or declaration of the professor that he or she will teach in communion with the Church can be expressed by the profession of faith and oath of fidelity or in any other reasonable manner acceptable to the one issuing the *mandatum*."[35]

I described the direct role of the university as very limited, but its indirect role is essential to its intended purpose. In simple terms, the university that considers itself Catholic must foster the cooperation of its Catholic theology professors with the local Church. Nonetheless, the *mandatum* serves an important purpose in theology, as described by the bishops in their *Guidelines Concerning the Academic Mandatum (Canon 812)*, issued in June 2001, by

> further[ing] that conversation [between bishops and administra-tors of Catholic universities] and build[ing] a community of trust and dialogue between Bishops and theologians. Without ongoing and respectful communication, the implementation of the *mandatum* might appear to be only a juridical constriction of the work of theologians.[36]

In other words, the *mandatum* indicates the important role theologians

---

[34] Ibid., sections 3, 4, and 5.

[35] Ibid., footnote 42.

[36] Found at www.usccb.org/beliefs-and-teachings/how-we-teach/catholic-education/ higher-education/guidelines-concerning-the-academic-mandatum.cfm.

exercise both in academia and in the Church and their obligation, as Catholic theologians, to remain in communion with the Church.

Quaestiones Disputatae

In the development of this article, I have become more convinced that the resolution of many issues affecting institutions of higher education calling themselves Catholic is fundamentally related to the clarification of an institution's precise canonical status. Such clarification means canonically implementing the changes that have already occurred through civil alienation and the establishment of statutes that articulate the precise status of the university in reference to the Church. It is only through clarification of its canonical status that university administrators may respond, positively and clearly, to specific questions about their Catholicity, their Catholic identity, and their use of the term Catholic.

On the more practical level, an institution that wishes to call itself Catholic cannot be so inclusive as to lose sight of its fundamental identity. Inclusiveness is necessary in academia but not inclusiveness to the point that the institution's Catholicity becomes simply one of numerous "identities" or "beliefs" allowed on campus. A Catholic university continuing to use the name Catholic or requesting its use from this point forward raises a number of canonical issues and perhaps civil issues as well. The following issues are not presented in any particular order:

The current *Code of Canon Law* requires that an undertaking or university that wishes to use the name Catholic in its title must secure the permission of the competent ecclesiastical authority. A new requirement in the code, without an equivalent in the prior code, the law is not retroactive, that is, on this basis alone the new norm does not pertain to institutions that have legitimately used "Catholic" previously in their self-description. The question could arise, therefore, that an institution that previously used the word Catholic has an "acquired right" to continue to use the word Catholic, that is, "a subjective right (*ius*) acquired in virtue of a juridical fact already performed and completed."[37]

While universities could assert an acquired right to the use of the term "Catholic"—that is, canon law experts could develop canonical arguments

---

[37] John Abbo and Jerome Hannan, *The Sacred Canons. A Concise Presentation of the Current Disciplinary Norms of the Church*, 2 vols. (St. Louis, MO: B. Herder, 1952), vol. 1, p. 7.

based on acquired rights against an ill-founded attempt to remove such usage—two points must be recognized. First, in reference to acquired rights, canon 4 states that such rights pertain to physical or juridic persons who as such are subject to canon law, thus expressly recognizing the applicability of Church law to the institution. Second, reconciling the application of an acquired right to the use of the word Catholic understood as "maintaining communion with the Church," especially an understanding of the Church as *communio* that highlights its dynamic, ongoing nature, would be an onerous task, if not impossible.

A second issue concerns the competent ecclesiastical authority that could allow use of the name "Catholic." Article 3 of *Ex Corde Ecclesiae*'s "General Norms" states:

§ 1. A Catholic University may be established or approved by the Holy See, by an Episcopal Conference or another Assembly of Catholic Hierarchy, or by a diocesan Bishop.

§ 2. With the consent of the diocesan Bishop, a Catholic University may also be established by a Religious Institute or other public juridical person.

§ 3. A Catholic University may also be established by other ecclesiastical or lay persons; such a University may refer to itself as a Catholic University only with the consent of the competent ecclesiastical Authority, in accordance with the conditions upon which both parties shall agree.

§ 4. In the cases of §§ 1 and 2, the Statutes must be approved by the competent ecclesiastical Authority.

Similarly, "The Application *of Ex Corde Ecclesiae*" requires a new Catholic university to "see to it that its canonical status is identified, including the ecclesiastical authority by which it has been established or approved or to which it otherwise relates" and that its statutes are approved "by competent ecclesiastical authority."[38]

---

[38] "The Application of *Ex Corde Ecclesiae*," Article 3.

The issue is much more complicated when questions concern Catholic universities established decades if not a century or more in the past. For example, some administrators have claimed that the universities had been alienated from a founding religious institute through the establishment of lay boards of trustees. But a person or an institution claiming to be Catholic is subject to two sets of laws: civil law and Church norms. Civil alienation does not necessarily have canonical effects; hence my argument that the canonical status of each institution would benefit from clarification of its canonical status. Further, the extent of civil alienation matters: does it refer only to property or to governance or does it include other aspects of the institution? For example, the argument could be made that alienation included alienation of the use of the name Catholic inasmuch as such usage originally derived from the religious institute, a juridic person in the Church, with rights and obligations.

If a competent ecclesiastical authority denied a university the continued use of "Catholic," the action would raise numerous questions that do not have easy answers. For example, if the institution does have juridic personality, its argument that it had an acquired right to the word "Catholic" would need canonical resolution. The authority would need to demonstrate the foundation in the law and in the facts of its decision and the decision would still be, as an exercise of executive authority, subject to hierarchical recourse.

More positively, communion with the competent ecclesiastical authority particularizes communion in the Church and does not leave it amorphous. Any physical or juridic person claiming to be Catholic and thus in a relationship with the Church must manifest its Catholicity by maintaining communion with the diocesan bishop and the particular church in which it is domiciled or located. This relationship cannot remain at an abstract and theoretical level but must find expression in every aspect of the life of the university. Leaving a university's canonical status undetermined can give rise to difficulties with the diocesan bishop while determining its canonical status tells it and its bishop the parameters of involvement on both sides.

Third, the extremely convoluted issue of ownership of the assets of a university must be settled case by case. A combination of expertise in civil law and canon law is needed to analyze the relevant documentation and to take due cognizance of the binding force of both systems of laws. For example, if a university had been recognized as a public juridic person in the Church through its establishment by a religious institute, itself a public juridic person, any claim in an ecclesiastical tribunal that the assets had been alienated civilly through the establishment of a civilly recognized corporation and a predominantly lay board of trustees could be countered by the juridic person of the religious institute arguing that its rights—that is, ownership of the property—had been violated through a canonically invalid alienation and consequently restitution to the institute must be given.[39]

The fourth issue is to what extent the adjective "Catholic" or "in the tradition of such and such religious institute" indicates a merely terminological homage to the historical foundations of a given institution or imbues the entire mission of the university in policy, in interaction with the local Church, in its public perception. Often the claim is made that an overtly Catholic identity would preclude the government funding necessary to the viability of the institution. This argument refuses to acknowledge the fact that a number of universities in the United States clearly and unequivocally manifest a very specific and overt religious affiliation while simultaneously accepting and using government funds. In these cases, Catholic identity becomes something negotiable, not essential to the university.

The following examples may seem to raise secondary issues, but I raise them precisely because the claim or assessment that these examples are secondary (or even trivial) can reveal much of the extent or the limit to which administrators wish to manifest Catholicity in the daily life of their institutions. If the university wishes to call itself Catholic, use of such terminology cannot simply be nominal; students must recognize that they are enrolling in a university founded on Catholic principles and life.

Are specifically Catholic activities—Masses, Lenten and Advent services, pro-life Masses—actively supported and attended by the university's higher administration or are they considered solely the domain of "campus ministry" and thus relegated to the fringe of the academic enterprise? The administration of a university that wants to describe itself as Catholic must indicate in action and not only in words that the Catholicity of the institution is essential and nonequivocal.

Further, in the interests of "openness" and "nonexclusivity," does the uni-

---

[39] See, for example, John Beal, "From the Heart of the Church," p. 37, note 12. In reference to the sale of Saint Louis University Hospital, he quotes the Congregation for Institutes of Consecrated Life and Societies of Apostolic Life, which stated that the owner of the hospital, ecclesiastically understood, was the Missouri Province of the Society of Jesus as a public juridic person of the Church.

versity adopt policies that, rather than welcome other religions and even atheists to a Catholic campus, give greater priority to non-Catholics than to Catholics and to the Catholic faith? Does it have a policy (official or unofficial) of not using the name of Jesus Christ in public prayers, so as not to be exclusive? Does it deny the competent authority any involvement or, at least, legitimate interest in its life? If the university does any of these, it has misunderstood the very nature of describing itself as Catholic. It is self-contradictory in its very identity. This is not canonically or civilly responsible.

In reference to mission statements of some Catholic universities, Michael Buckley has written:

> [I]t is precisely when such institutions have allowed the Catholic character of their education to be subsumed by contextual references to a religious heritage, by general phrases that bespeak this tradition but remain unspecified for American higher education and by moralisms that any enlightened figure would applaud, then one who admires them and hopes for great things from them cannot but suspect some decline at least in collective vision. This seems to me an enormously serious situation.[40]

The mission statements to which he refers are problematic in and of themselves to any university that considers itself Catholic. I would argue further that such generic mission statements are replacing or have replaced any concept of maintaining communion with the Church.

These exemplar issues—contemporary and continued usage of the word Catholic; determination of the competent ecclesiastical authority to allow or deny the use of Catholic as self-descriptive; clarification of the issue of asset and liability ownership; the question of whether or not the word Catholic is used by a university without all dimensions of the academic enterprise manifesting its implications—are necessarily limited and particular. While other examples could be discussed, these at least indicate the range of issues confronting an institution that claims to be Catholic.

---

[40] Michael Buckley, "The Catholic University and the Promise Inherent in Its Identity," in *Catholic Universities in Church and Society. A Dialogue on* Ex Corde Ecclesiae, edited by John Langan and Leo O'Donovan (Washington, D.C.: Georgetown University Press, 1993), p. 79.

Conclusion

Rather than addressing a false dichotomy between faith and reason, we might need to address the real dichotomy: a dichotomy between faith and practice, as evidenced in the following quotation:

> It is no less clear that today, in traditionally Christian nations, secular institutions, although demonstrating a high degree of scientific and technical perfection, and efficiency in achieving their respective ends, not infrequently are but slightly affected by Christian motivation or inspiration. It is beyond question that in the creation of those institutions many contributed and continue to contribute who were believed to be and who consider themselves Christians; and without doubt, in part at least, they were and are. How does one explain this? It is [my] opinion that the explanation is to be found in an inconsistency in their minds between religious belief and their action in the temporal sphere [*agendi ratio cum sua fide non cohaereat*]. It is necessary, therefore, that their interior unity be reestablished, and that in their temporal activity Faith should be present as a beacon to give light, and Charity as a force to give life. [41]

Agendi ratio cum sua fide non cohaereat. The most dangerous dichotomy is not between a Catholic university and the Catholic Church, or between the magisterium and a theological faculty, or even between faith and reason, but the often obvious dichotomy between belief and praxis.

The quotation above, as noted, is taken from Pope St. John XXIII's pivotal encyclical *Pacem in Terris*, published in 1963. By focusing on ancillary issues, we avoid the fundamental responsibility: the degree to which we allow our faith to determine our lives and actions, and more specifically, in reference to the topic of this paper, the degree to which a Catholic university and its administration recognize that its faith is essential to its foundation as well as to its ongoing presence as a vital academic force. As a Catholic institution, at least in description, the Catholic faith must necessarily determine its policy; must direct relationships among its faculty, staff, students, and administra-

---

[41] Pope John XXIII, *Pacem in Terris* (Washington, D.C.: National Catholic Welfare Conference, 1963), p. 151–152.

tion; must refer to its relationship with its founding institute or group or bishop and its relationship to the local Church.

The university that describes itself as Catholic must, as each Catholic must do, express one's faith in and through actions. In the words of *Lumen Gentium*:

> That person is not saved [*non salvatur*], however, who, even though he might be incorporated into the Church, who does not persevere in charity; he does indeed remain in the bosom of the Church, but "bodily" but not "in his heart."[42]

The question, then, confronting a university that claims to be Catholic is the following: To what extent does a university claiming to be Catholic remain in the heart of the Church as opposed to simply existing there in a bodily manner?

---

[42] *Lumen Gentium* 14 in *Decrees of the Ecumenical Councils*, vol. 2, p. 860.

Leadership in Catholic Higher Education

JAMES L. HEFT, S.M.

ALTON M. BROOKS PROFESSOR OF RELIGION,

UNIVERSITY OF SOUTHERN CALIFORNIA

A member of the board of trustees of Yale in the 19th century described the qualities of the person they were seeking to fill the position of president (forgive the patriarchy and sexism of the description): "He had to be a good leader, a magnificent speaker, a great writer, a good public relations man, a man of iron health and stamina, married to a paragon of virtue. His wife, in fact, had to be a mixture of Queen Victoria, Florence Nightingale and the best dressed woman of the year. We saw our choice as having to be a man of the world, but an individual with great spiritual qualities; an experienced administrator, but able to delegate; a Yale man, and a great scholar; a social philosopher, who though he had the solutions to the world's problems, has still not lost the common touch. After lengthy deliberation, we concluded that there was only one such person. But then a dark thought crossed our minds. We had to ask—is God a Yale man?"[1]

Despite the extraordinary diversity among Catholic colleges and universities, most institutions still draw up very similar descriptions of the person they want to be their president—descriptions that few humans could fulfill. Presidents must be charismatic, accomplished administrators, fund-raisers, moral exemplars, crisis managers, scholars, accessible to faculty, and skilled in dealing with the local bishop. No one person, however talented he or she may be, will meet even half those expectations thrust upon them by multiple

---

[1] Frank Rhodes, *The Creation of the Future* (Ithaca, NY: Cornell University Press, 2001), p. 222.

audiences, especially as presidents of Catholic colleges and universities face such formidable challenges. Are there good resources and models for presidents to draw on to meet these challenges? Are there effective ways to prepare individuals for leadership in these special institutions?

The few authors who address university leadership write little about Catholic institutions. They do not address the unique issues that presidents of Catholic colleges and universities face. One exception, *Lay Leaders in Catholic Higher Education,* deals directly with our topic.[2] Many of the essays in the book comment on a survey, now 10 years old, designed by Fr. Dennis Holtschneider, C.M., and Melanie Morey. Last year, the Association of Catholic Colleges and Universities (ACCU) and Boston College (BC) cosponsored a new survey of presidents. The results of these surveys form the baseline of data to which I will frequently refer in this paper. I will also draw upon Cardinal Newman's *Idea of a University,* and cite some relevant advice offered by the few Catholic university presidents who have written about their experiences. Finally, based on my own 14-year experience as an administrator in a major Catholic university, I will also describe how, at least at one Catholic university, we attempted to meet some of the major challenges I describe in the first half of this paper.

Secularization and Commercialization

First, cultural changes beyond the university have profoundly influenced Catholic universities. Evaluations of these changes have varied greatly (see, for example, James Burtchaell, George Marsden, Brad Gregory, Melanie Morey and John Piderit, S.J., Alice Gallin, O.S.U., Michael Baxter and Frederick C. Bauerschmidt, and David O'Brien).[3] They all agree, however, that profound changes have transformed the academy. Not the least of these changes has been the increasing commercialization and secularization of American culture, which has bled over into Catholic higher education.

---

[2]   *Lay Leaders in Catholic Higher Education,* edited by Anthony Cernera (Fairfield, CT: Sacred Heart University Press, 2005).

[3]   James Burtchaell, *The Dying of the Light: The Disengagement of Colleges and Universities from Their Christian Churches* (Grand Rapids, MI: Eerdmans, 1998), see my review in *Catholic Education: A Journal of Inquiry and Practice* 2, no. 4 (June 1991), pp. 495–503; George Marsden, *The Soul of the American University* (New York: Oxford, 1994); Brad Gregory, *The Unintended Reformation: How a Religious Revolution Secularized Society* (Cambridge, MA: Harvard University Press, 2012); and Michael Baxter and Frederick Bauerschmidt, "Eruditio without Religio: The Dilemma of Catholics in the Academy," *Communio* 22 (Summer 1995), pp. 284–302.

Until the 1950s, most Catholic colleges and universities succeeded in sealing themselves off from many of these changes. Since then, however, in the spirit of the Second Vatican Council, they opened themselves to the wider culture, welcomed greater diversity, professionalized their faculty, became more autonomous, and benefited from sizable amounts of government funding. Though these institutions always prepared their graduates to make a living, the degree to which secularization and commercialism now shape colleges and universities is unprecedented.

Moreover, the phenomenon of secularization is multifaceted. It created more room for independent thinking, for a distinction between secular and ecclesial authorities, and, within the Catholic tradition, affirmed more clearly the autonomy of the sciences. At the same time, however, the general academic culture is now less religious than that of the general population. Within Catholic universities, some faculty minimize, at times even trivialize, the contributions that a religious tradition can make to the intellectual life. The religious tradition is relegated to a few disciplines and identified with campus ministry.

These sweeping changes, which began after the Civil War, gained warp speed after World War II, even though nearly all the first American colleges were founded as religious institutions. Because of the tendency today that ignores the original religious inspiration of the vast majority of the institutions that were once proud of their religious affiliation, leaders in Catholic higher education need to be especially explicit, and proud, of the religious inspiration of their institutions.

The Catholic Dimension

When they designed their survey, Holtschneider and Morey assumed that an effective leader of a Catholic university needed to have had at least some courses in theology and philosophy. They were surprised, however, when they learned that few of their respondents thought such courses were relevant for them. Alice Hayes, a biologist and once president of the University of San Diego, commented on the researchers' surprise:

> The preparation that Morey and Holtschneider have measured is the preparation to be a religious, not preparation to be a university president. They observe that a religious is "granted moral credibility and leadership through the structure of vows or ordination."

> There is no doubt that this happens, but as we have learned in
> recent years, ordination no more assures the moral credibility of
> a priest than baptism does for a lay person. I do not think that it
> is necessary or appropriate to prepare for leadership of a Catholic
> university in the same way as one would prepare to be a sister,
> brother or priest.[4]

Whether such courses would adequately prepare someone for the presidency is, of course, debatable. Nevertheless, it needs to be asked what level of knowledge and familiarity a person needs to have with the institution's religious tradition to be qualified to lead an academic community at the university level. How many of our universities, especially those founded by religious orders, prepare their leaders by offering the appropriate theological and spiritual formation. Only in recent years has appropriate theological formation been developed for leaders, and then only rarely. More often, despite inflated expectations, most searches, whatever their many expectations of a president may be, give priority to fund-raising or management skills.

The ACCU/BC survey (the survey appears as Appendix A.) asked presidents how they dealt with the "Catholic dimension" and how much they thought their campus constituents understood and promoted it. The survey did not ask what they understood by the "Catholic dimension," but John Langan, S.J., described the Catholic dimension presidents have to deal with:

> [T]the content of theology and philosophy courses, the behavior
> tolerated or forbidden in residence halls, the interpretation and
> fulfillment of the academic and religious commitment to social
> justice and community service, the choice of candidates for
> honorary degrees, the sorts of speakers who appear on campus
> [as well as the] relationships with Church authorities...and
> priorities the faculty brings to the task of choosing and hiring
> its own members.[5]

Unless someone complains about a professor of philosophy or theology, the other issues mentioned can easily consume nearly all of the president's time

---

[4] Cernera, *Lay Leaders in Catholic Higher Education*, pp. 40–41.

[5] Ibid., pp. 144–145.

and energy. To meet the challenges posed by those who disregard or ignore the "Catholic dimension" requires, as we shall see, a rich understanding of it, especially as it should shape an academic institution.

The Faculty Challenge

In both surveys, presidents indicated that one of their biggest challenges was dealing with the faculty. They reported that not many faculty really helped students understand the "Catholic dimension." The first survey stated that "both lay and religious report that the faculty is an obstacle to effective leadership in the area of Catholic character, mission and identity."[6] Some 10 years later, the ACCU/BC survey shows that nothing has changed. The faculty contribute least to the "Catholic dimension" of the life of their institution—a sobering assessment, especially when you consider that faculty have tenure, outlive administrators, shape the curriculum, and interact daily with students. A faculty that contributes little to the Catholic dimension poses a most serious challenge for presidents.

Moreover, it hardly helps matters that few faculty think of the Catholic intellectual tradition as a resource that enriches their intellectual life. At secular universities, many faculty operate with this bias, or should I say, prejudice. University of Virginia professor Robert Louis Wilken recently wrote that when it comes to the intellectual life, Catholic scholars at secular universities hide the lamp of Catholic thought under a bushel:

> An occasional faculty member, or a group of students, will join in a protest against abortion, but in public discussion and debate it is rare to find a Catholic professor addressing the issues in a distinctively Catholic way. The Catholic presence runs the gamut from pizza at a Newman Center event to community service, but it seldom reaches into the library or lecture hall. Piety is evident. Catholic intellect and learning are not....More often their Catholicism is a private and personal thing, an affair of piety and practice, divorced from the intellectual enterprise that is the business of the university.[7]

---

[6] Ibid., p. 17.

[7] Robert Louis Wilken, "Catholic Scholars, Secular Schools," *First Things* (January 2008), p. 40.

To what extent is the situation described by Wilken also true of faculty at Catholic universities? If it is true, what can be done about it? Obviously, presidents need to think long and hard about how they might address challenges posed by the faculty.

The Dominance of Science

Presidents of Catholic universities face still another major challenge, the dominance of science. The Catholic intellectual tradition, rightly understood, has no difficulty with science, when science limits its conclusions to what can be known through an empirical exploration of nature. The problem, rather, is *scientism*, that is, the assumption that science creates the only reliable and ultimate explanation of *all* reality. *Scientism* diminishes the role of the humanities. Humanists understand that all that counts is not countable and good scientists do as well. The scientific method is not the problem; rather, it is scientists who think science is a metaphysics that explains everything (not even good philosophers assume that metaphysics explains everything!). Even scientists who are not full-blown proponents of *scientism* sometimes dismiss less empirical methods of doing research.

In the words of Denys Turner, these professors "reverse the traffic between questions and answers so as to permit only such questions to be asked as they already possess predetermined methodologies for answering, cutting the agenda of questions down to the shape and size of their given routines for answering them." For them, theology and metaphysics are irrelevant. When faculty at any university, and especially faculty at a Catholic university, value only the empirical approach, their attitude spells the death not only of the liberal arts, but of every discipline—and certainly the intellectual death of a Catholic university—which should be asking unanswerable questions, even of God.

On the other hand, too many humanities faculty understand very little of the sciences and social sciences. Some humanities professors—often philosophers and theologians—talk about the "Catholic dimension" in ways that leave the scientists scratching their heads. The language in which they conduct that conversation seems to scientists strange, even impenetrable. Scientists then conclude that whatever the "Catholic dimension" is, it ought to stay within the humanities.

Social scientists and faculty in the professions may feel the same as the scientists. Humanities faculty need to remember that the social sciences illuminate human behavior as it unfolds on the ground, while the professions apply knowledge. Professors in the humanities can no more afford to be ignorant of the findings of the social sciences and the sciences than the latter can be dismissive of the light shed upon the human condition by the humanities. Fostering substantive conversations about Catholicism as an intellectual resource for all the faculty is, therefore, as important to accomplish as it is difficult to do. Leaders in Catholic universities should give top priority to fostering this conversation among their faculty.

The Challenge of Commercialization

Commercialization weakens the "Catholic dimension." It pushes leaders to commodify everything, to think of the university as a business, to turn faculty into bargaining units, and students into consumers. Even though already at the time of the birth of the university in the Middle Ages the professions of law, the ministry, and medicine held a prominent place, they never displaced theology and philosophy. Given the extraordinary influence of today's market economy, presidents need to be especially vigilant to avoid pressures, sometimes exerted by boards of trustees, to maximize revenue, bureaucratize all transactions, and think of faculty as "employees" and students as "customers." Development and public relations staff, which usually report directly to the president, abet commercialization when they reduce the mission of the university to what is popular and sells.

A Catholic university is about more than a good margin, as important as that is. Is margin always more important than mission? How much time do presidents spend worrying about finances compared to worrying about the intellectual and spiritual vitality of their institutions? Unfortunately, most focus most of their energy securing the financial well-being of their institutions. They need also to focus regularly and profoundly on the distinctively religious and intellectual mission of their institutions. How many boards of trustees hold their presidents accountable for strengthening the Catholic intellectual life of the faculty?

Multiple—Sometimes Antagonistic—Audiences

Presidents address very different audiences. They live simultaneously in many different worlds; they need to be amphibians. In one world, that of parents, donors, prospective students, and bishops, they send positive messages of strength, safety, quality, and religious fidelity. This audience receives publications that are peppered with words like "transformational, catalytic, innovative, out of the box, game changer" and "warm," "supportive," "ortho-dox," and attentive to the "whole person." Their publications feature the latest information technology, sophisticated science labs, and dynamic entrepre-neur programs. They boast of how quickly their graduates find jobs and their alums succeed in business. Glossy photos show sparkling student residences and the new student center and recreation facilities, enjoyed by smiling students who represent "diversity."

That is one world—the one that hears the best about the institution. There is another world, however, the "inside" world where the president often faces faculty who are suspicious of too much emphasis on Catholicism, who com-plain about unprepared students, who criticize hiring too many non-tenure-line faculty, who oppose unilateral financial decisions, imposed hiring freez-es, and excessive spending on sports and recreational facilities. And if these criticisms aren't enough, what needs to be done with students who drink and party too much?

The picture painted for the external audience contrasts, sometimes sharp-ly, with the reality the presidents face internally. How can presidents deal with these very different worlds and communicate forthrightly and appropriately with both? How public can presidents afford to be about problems when their institutions are in competition, sometimes for their very existence, with other Catholic colleges and universities?

Still another world is the presidents' families or their religious community. How to avoid burnout, find enough time for family (or a proper engagement with their community), and find the time to exercise—these are the real issues many presidents struggle with. Would a spiritual director help, or a physical trainer, and a board that requires that their president take at least a one-month vacation away from campus?

The Challenge of the Culture Wars

Besides dealing with the different worlds, presidents also need to deal with graduates who think they know best what a Catholic university should be. This challenge is a subset of the Catholic "culture wars." The media lionizes vocal liberals and especially conservatives; presidents become defensive. Some Catholics see as the only issues abortion and homosexuality; others dedicate themselves to issues of justice and poverty. Both groups fall into different forms of "cafeteria Catholicism." Not surprisingly, then, people on the left and right have very different ideas as to what constitutes a "real" Catholic university.

It gets even more complicated when leaders of Catholic universities differ significantly on what constitutes a "real" Catholic university. For example, in a recent newsletter, one lay president of what might be described as a conservative small Catholic college wrote that the devastating effects of the 1960s continues to "infect" most Catholic colleges and universities so that now they, as clearly distinguished from his own institution, have adopted the "diluted curricula, methods, and aims of their secular counterparts," and have "succumbed to the permissiveness of the time," allowing "a longstanding commitment to Catholic liberal education" to disappear. The source of this academic apostasy is, according to this president, the 1967 "Land O'Lakes" statement drafted by a group of Catholic educators led by Notre Dame's Fr. Theodore Hesburgh, which he believed reversed the tradition in which the "measure of the Catholic university was the *magisterium* of the Church." Now, in his view, the Catholic university is not only its own measure, but also presumes to be the measure of the Church. At this president's campus, bishops and cardinals speak at all the graduation ceremonies, and lend legitimacy to the president's leadership and vision of Catholicism.

Conservative Catholic institutions have difficulty with pluralism, liberal ones with the "Catholic dimension." Conservative institutions invite only speakers who fully support the current official teachings of the Church. Less conservative Catholic institutions welcome speakers with diverse views, even some who support only some of the official teachings of the Catholic Church. Leaders of liberal institutions believe that the very conservative institutions run the risk of creating an artificial religious bubble that will not prepare their graduates for the "real" world. On the other hand, leaders of the liberal institutions who support a diversity of views may fail to present clearly the Catholic tradition. Liberals hope that students will learn more about the Catholic faith by witnessing a dialogue between a Catholic member of their faculty and persons of a different faith. How many Catholic faculty are willing and competent to engage in such a dialogue? One wonders if the answer to that question can be confidently positive when the BC/ACCU survey found that presidents report that they are unable to rely on faculty to promote their institution's Catholic character and mission. How confidentially can presidents defend their own institution's commitment to Catholicism?

The Challenge of Few Religious

Over 90 percent of Catholic colleges and universities have been founded by religious orders. Since the 1960s, their membership has dropped dramatically. How should presidents, both lay and religious, deal with the issues that typically arise from the absence of so many religious? How does a lay president go about assessing the degree to which the order's founding charism contributes to the ethos of the institution? In an earlier and quite different era of Catholicism, the very presence of sisters, brothers, and priests made the Catholicity of an institution clear. As Fr. Joseph Appleyard pointed out in a recent paper, "the strong internal culture of religious orders, central authority structure, and easily regulated doctrine and behavioral discipline" kept the identity of their Catholic institution clear.

What could be done now to make that Catholicity more evident? In the past, given the large numbers of religious and priests, people took for granted that the university was Catholic. On the other hand, in the past they may have felt little need to explore the nature of Catholic identity; they may even have felt less freedom to explore it. Today, in a time of tectonic cultural shifts, it is difficult to avoid the question of Catholic identity, especially when the Catholic population and bishops are often polarized about that very question.

The precipitous drop in the number of religious in these institutions shows no signs of turning around. Of the handful of new members, few seem interested in preparing for faculty positions or administration; some of them actually find resistance from faculty hiring committees—resistance in the very institution that their order founded and built over the decades. More lay presidents are leading these institutions. The 2002 survey documented that nearly 60 percent of presidents are lay. That percentage has surely increased since then. The authors of the survey claim that, with the increased number of lay presidents, "the once well-established pipeline and preparation process for leadership became less well-defined, less certain."[8] In the past, however, the preparation for religious to take on such positions was usually not "well established." Provincials sometimes abruptly appointed to the presidency a member of their own congregation who may have had no administrative experience (though some of them did quite well). That was then; now there is a long search process guided by professional consultants. The challenge of succession planning remains acute, especially when search firms, search

---

[8] Cernera, *Lay Leaders in Catholic Higher Education*, p. 3.

committees, and board leadership have little understanding of the critical importance of the Catholic mission of the institution.

Related to the question of the diminishing number of religious, what do presidents do when the founding order has increasing difficulty finding religious capable of serving on their university's board? Also, does it make sense that a religious always head the board's committee on mission? Would it not be better to appoint lay persons to head such committees?

Given that the topics of finances, enrollment, fund-raising, and buildings dominate most board meetings, what should a president do to ensure that the intellectual and religious mission of the institution also receives proper attention? If the business and management questions take up nearly all the time, the members of the board who are religious in effect become mascots rather than persons of real influence. Imagine also the unfortunate but not impossible scenario in which the head of the founding religious order tells the lay president that in the future, no religious will be assigned to their institution. In such a situation, how should a president go about deepening the founding order's charism? Finally, with fewer and fewer religious involved in the universities they've founded, it becomes increasingly difficult for the leaders of the religious communities to understand the complex workings of a university.

The Challenge of Relating to the Hierarchy

The potential for "gown and chancery" tensions has increased in recent years. In the past, when most of the presidents were religious and priests—when there was no tenure and little faculty governance—such tensions could be resolved through a more clericalized link with bishops. Few presidents ever invited controversial persons to receive honorary degrees; polarized views of Catholicism did not complicate matters to the extent that they do now. How should lay presidents, somewhat removed from the clerical world, deal with bishops when campus controversies erupt?

The public censoring of theologians, widely covered by the media, creates special challenges. In 1999, when a second attempt of the American bishops to apply *Ex Corde Ecclesiae* was finally approved, the Vatican required a juridical element, the *mandatum,* for theologians. This requirement created considerable anxiety among most theologians. Although *Ex Corde Ecclesiae* supports academic freedom "properly" understood, precisely what that proper understanding is remains a matter of debate among both theologians and bishops.

If the local bishop often assumes an adversarial position, the recruitment of faculty becomes more difficult. How should presidents protect the necessary academic freedom of theologians while at the same time maintaining a cordial relationship with the local bishop?

Selection and Formation of Boards of Trustees

Presidents who wish to strengthen the Catholic character of their institutions need board members who understand and support the "Catholic dimension." Several criteria should guide the selection of board members: support for the distinctive mission of the institution; willingness to devote time and treasure to the achievement of that mission; and a commitment to protect the institutions from excessive commercialization and secularization. Presidents should be as careful and dedicated in the selection of board members as athletic coaches are about the recruitment of athletes. Coaches know that if they do not recruit well, their job will be in jeopardy by the end of a single season.

What are some "best practices" for selecting and forming board members? As mentioned before, presidents need to ensure the formation of board members as to the nature of a university and the mission of a Catholic one, otherwise, the mission committee fights a losing battle to get airtime to make their contribution. How much time is spent on board formation?

A Summary of the Challenges

In the preceding pages I have taken the liberty to identify many of the challenges that face anyone who aspires to lead Catholic colleges and universities today. Given the great diversity of Catholic colleges and universities, it is impossible to address all the possible variations these challenges take. Nevertheless, it is to some practical consideration of ways they can and have been successfully addressed that I now turn.

Both surveys make it clear that the presidents face two key challenges (among others): first, understanding and strengthening the "Catholic dimension" as it relates to the disciplines, and second, hiring and forming faculty who support and develop that distinctive mission. Before addressing these issues directly, I turn to a mid-19th-century Catholic genius whose relevance is especially important today.

Newman's Vision of the Catholic University

In my estimation, Blessed John Henry Newman's writings, especially his

Idea of a University, remain a classic resource for understanding the "Catholic dimension" of the university. Originally given in Ireland in the 1850s as a series of lectures on liberal education, Newman eloquently described the mission of a Catholic university. Admittedly, the challenges Newman faced in the 1850s in Ireland are different from what Catholic university presidents face today. What then does Newman have to say that will be helpful to today's leaders of Catholic universities? Three of his contributions may be even more relevant today than they were in his own day: first, a compelling vision of the Catholic university; second, an emphasis on the critical importance of the formation of students; and third, a deep understanding of the proper relationship of the university to the hierarchy.

First, I believe Newman succeeds in presenting a compelling and coherent vision of a Catholic university education, especially important given the current power of secularization and commercialization in higher education. Presidents should study that vision, both for its content and style, even if today's context differs from Newman's. Newman makes it clear that if Catholic colleges and universities do not have a strong liberal arts program, they cannot claim to be Catholic. It is ironic, even embarrassing, that some secular liberal arts colleges offer a better liberal education than most of our Catholic colleges and universities. What Catholic college or university has a reputation for the study of languages and the classics? Leaders of Catholic colleges could learn from their programs.

For Newman, two disciplines in particular were central to his vision of a liberal education: philosophy and theology. When theology is absent from the curriculum, Newman writes, some other subject fills that vacuum and assumes its role. Philosophy appropriately connects and orders all the other subjects. Today, no secular university would hire a theologian, and philosophers at secular universities rarely worry about the proper ordering of the rest of the disciplines.

We live in a highly commercialized age. The "prestige ratings" published annually in *Newsweek* depend primarily on quantitative measurements: acceptance rates, endowments, library holdings, and student-teacher ratios. How can the liberal arts be quantitatively evaluated? In a commercialized society, the prestige of the liberal arts falls considerably below that of the professions and the sciences (unless a major company needs people who can read and write!). It is, of course, difficult for those Catholic colleges and universities that are fighting for survival to ignore completely such ratings. The market economy's pervasive influence also contributes to the wide gap that exists among faculty salaries. External funding for research in the humanities pales by comparison to that available to engineers, scientists, and business professors. These "market" factors—prestige ratings, faculty salaries, and research support—push students, to the relief of many parents, away from majoring in philosophy or theology.

In Catholic institutions, faculties of philosophy and theology, as well as English and history, are required to meet core requirements, which means multiple lower-level classes, all filled with mostly non-humanities majors. Few students who major in the humanities turn out to become wealthy donors. Because philosophers and theologians are also not well compensated compared to business, medical, or law professors, they rarely enjoy much influence on campus. On some campuses, philosophers and theologians have to fend off efforts by curriculum committees to reduce the number of their required courses. In view of these pressures, both external and internal, Newman challenges the leaders of Catholic universities to give strong support to the liberal arts, especially to philosophy and theology—not to mention art, music, and drama, fields of special importance for a religious tradition that values liturgy and sacraments.

Newman and Student Formation

Second, Newman places the formation of the student at the heart of education. Clark Kerr once described Newman's educational vision as "bucolic," as representing "the beautiful ivory tower of Oxford as it once was," relevant only for elite undergraduates who live in small colleges.[9] He contrasted Newman's college with the German model of graduate education—a model that he believed, for the purposes of research, was more dynamic and relevant today than a liberal arts college. Most universities assume that graduate students are already formed, and just need to learn how to do research. We know better: formation is lifelong.

Newman, however, stresses the importance of the moral formation of students, both undergraduate and graduate. He emphasized the close personal relationship between the students and their mentors. Large Catholic universities with over 10,000 students and an investment in graduate education need most to remember this part of Newman's vision of education.

---

[9]   Clark Kerr, *The Uses of the University* (Cambridge, MA: Harvard University Press, 2001), p. 95.

Newman's Plea for "Elbow Room"

The third lesson Newman teaches us addresses the sometimes difficult relationship between the university and the hierarchy. The bishops of Ireland had invited Newman to establish a university, but from the outset frustrated him. They really wanted a seminary, not a university. In response to a request for advice from a Jesuit priest, Bartholomew Woodlock, who followed him as president of the Irish Catholic University, Newman wrote: "It is my duty, when you, as head of the University, ask my mind, to give it, and I do so, but I don't wish what I say repeated." After assuring Woodlock that there was indeed talent sufficient to "accept the great venture of a real Catholic University," he added: "On the other hand, it is *essential* that the Church should have a living presence and control in the action of the University. But still, till the bishops leave the University to itself, till the University governs itself, till it is able to act as a free being, it will be but a sickly child."[10]

Ex Corde Ecclesiae does better in understanding the role of bishops than did Newman's Irish bishops. It gives support to a real university, not a seminary. It does not claim for bishops any direct role in the running of Catholic colleges and universities, and grants to universities institutional autonomy and academic freedom, "properly" understood. Newman actually anticipated much of *Ex Corde Ecclesiae*. In fact, in some ways, he goes beyond it. As a Catholic, he often complained that bishops held theologians on a short leash. If theologians render real service to their students and to the Church, Newman insisted they be given "elbow room."

A student of history, Newman knew that the relationship between bishops and theologians could be tense. Occasionally, a bishop is a good theologian, but ordinarily not. Bishops and theologians have different tasks. Theologians can deeply influence the thinking of bishops (just think of Vatican II), just as bishops can influence the work of theologians (again, think of Vatican II). Both bishops and theologians need to be attentive to the "signs of the times" and be guided by the faith of the entire Church. The *magisterium* is not superior to the Word of God, but its servant, as *Dei Verbum* noted. And in the last analysis, the faith of the entire Church is strengthened by the work of theologians who have the elbow room to explore.

For the first time in history, the 1983 revised *Code of Canon Law* contains

---

[10] John Henry Newman, *Letters and Diaries*, vol. 24 (New York: Oxford University Press, 1973), p. 46.

a section on higher education. Several years later, and at much greater length, Pope John Paul II's 1990 Apostolic Exhortation, *Ex Corde Ecclesiae,* spells out the nature and mission of non-pontifically chartered Catholic colleges and universities. Newman's vision of a Catholic university enriches both these sources.

In the early 1980s, Cardinal Yves Congar wrote that all theological research should focus not on infallibility (the *magisterium*), but on "life in the truth of Christ (1 Cor. 12:3)." When interpreting documents issued by the *magisterium,* theologians need to go "beyond a naïve reading" and instead present a "maturely critical understanding and a re-rendering that meets the needs of the educated world today.""" He also gives great importance to the faith of the whole Church, the *sensus fidelium,* often most visible in the practice of the faithful, especially in situations of oppression and injustice, and above all in the witness of martyrs: "The blood of witnesses guarantees the seriousness involved." A "maturely critical understanding" is not simply the repetition of the *Catechism.* How can a president of a university at one and the same time protect the academic freedom of theologians, support the expectation of a *mandatum* called for by *Ex Corde Ecclesiae,* and remain in a necessary and vital relationship with the larger Church?

Because he transcends the polarization so evident in our culture wars, stresses the moral and intellectual formation of students, and supports the important role of the humanities, which safeguards what is distinctive about Catholic higher education, Newman remains relevant for today's leaders of Catholic colleges and universities.

Acquiring a Richer Understanding of the Catholic Dimension

Catholicism makes significant claims, both religious and intellectual, claims that are relevant to the disciplines. Presidents need to understand the overall shape of Catholic intellectual tradition, which embraces much more than theology and philosophy.

As a tradition, Catholicism is best understood as an ongoing conversation, sometimes contentious, regularly multifaceted, globally and culturally diverse, embodying and searching for what is good and true and beautiful in all of reality. Catholicism poses a distinctive set of questions and affirms

---

[11] Yves Congar, "Towards a Catholic Synthesis," in *Concilium: Who Has the Say in the Church?* edited by Jürgen Moltmann and Hans Küng (New York: Seabury Press, 1981), p. 69.

certain truths that stress the transcendent character of the human person, created in the image and likeness of God. Catholicism emphasizes the importance of community, of liturgical and sacramental practices, philosophical thought that is open to religious questions and theological reflection that welcomes rational inquiry. Catholicism affirms the doctrine of creation, and therefore fosters a nonmaterialist but fully empirical approach to the natural and social sciences. In a word, Catholicism embraces all of reality.

Light can also be shed on the nature of the Catholic tradition from an angle different than that of a historian and a theologian. Poet and literary critic Dana Gioia, writing about Catholic writers, describes their worldview in this way: "There is no singular and uniform Catholic worldview, but nevertheless it is possible to describe some general characteristics that encompass both the faithful and the renegade among the literati," he writes.

> Catholic writers tend to see humanity struggling in a fallen world. They combine a longing for grace and redemption with a deep sense of human imperfection and sin. Evil exists, but the physical world is not evil. Nature is sacramental, shimmering with signs of sacred things. Indeed, all reality is mysteriously charged with the invisible presence of God. Catholics perceive suffering as redemptive, at least when borne in emulation of Christ's passion and death. Catholics also generally take the long view of things—looking back to the time of Christ and the Caesars while also gazing forward toward eternity. (The Latinity of the pre-Vatican II Church sustained a meaningful continuity with the ancient Roman world, reaching even into working-class Los Angeles of the 1960s, where I was raised and educated.) Catholicism is also intrinsically communal, a notion that goes far beyond sitting at Mass with the local congregation, extending to a mystical sense of continuity between the living and the dead. Finally, there is a habit of spiritual self-scrutiny and moral examination of conscience—one source of *soi-disant* Catholic guilt.[12]

The breadth of Catholic tradition may also be seen in its sophisticated tradition of social ethics, especially valuable for professional education. One does

---

[12]   Dana Gioia, "The Catholic Writer Today," *First Things* (December 2013), pp. 34–35.

not have to be Catholic or a Christian to appreciate these ethical teachings. The Catholic intellectual tradition is most visible when it is integrated with ethical practices rooted in a living faith. In other words, a Catholic intellectual needs to live the faith tradition. Any Catholic university would do well to make sure that among their strongest and most respected scholars are committed Catholics. Pope Paul VI once remarked that students listen to witnesses, not just teachers—but most of all, they listen to teachers who witness.

Hiring and Working with the Faculty

As important as theologians and philosophers are for the Catholic university, it is the entire faculty that, in ways appropriate to their disciplines, bears the responsibility for the "Catholic dimension" of the institution. One of the benefits of multiple disciplinary programs called "Catholic Studies" is that they show that the Catholic intellectual tradition includes more than theology and philosophy.[13]

How can a president influence the hiring of faculty? If the president or provost were to announce at a faculty meeting that in the future they plan to hire faculty who support the "Catholic dimension," the majority of faculty would, I believe, object. After all, faculty, not administrators, hire faculty. Some faculty might conclude that the administration has been coerced by the bishop or rich donors to promote narrow Catholic ideology instead of academic quality. They may fear that such a policy will end their efforts to hire a diverse faculty. Even faculty sympathetic to the Catholic tradition sometimes feel torn between hiring faculty who support the Catholic mission and hiring academically qualified faculty. Despite such objections and tensions, leadership needs to pay careful attention to the university's mission in the hiring process, or run the risk of locating its "Catholicity" only in the office of the presidency, a single mission officer, and the campus ministry program. How, then, should academic leaders tackle this volatile challenge?

Unfortunately, the issues—Catholic identity and diversity—are seldom understood in ways that strengthen both Catholic identity and improve academic quality. The conflict is most acute when hiring committees assume either that they should hire only Catholics, or that they should hire people of

---

[13]   See *The Catholic Studies Reader*, edited by James T. Fisher and Margaret M. McGuinness (Bronx, NY: Fordham University Press, 2011). See also Thomas M. Landy, "Catholic Studies at Catholic Colleges and Universities," *America* (January 3, 1998).

color or some other minority category regardless of how well that person will contribute to the mission. Some faculty do not feel conflict because they redefine "Catholic" as meaning universal; they welcome everyone. At universities founded by religious orders, faculty have been known to downplay the Catholic dimension, and instead emphasize the mission of the founding religious order in terms of inclusiveness and collaboration. In hiring, then, they forefront academic competence and diversity while paying less, and sometimes no, attention to mission.

When a more dynamic understanding of Catholic intellectual life guides the search committee, it will no longer be necessary to think that increasing faculty diversity means downplaying the university's Catholic mission. Properly understood, Catholic inclusivity does welcome everyone, regardless of race, creed, or color, as long as they can in their own way and discipline contribute to the university's distinctive intellectual commitments.

One Example of "Hiring for Mission"

There is, of course, no one best way to undertake this important task. But I think it would prove helpful for me to describe in some detail one example of how to go about hiring that seems to be bearing fruit. In the early 1980s, while serving as chair of the Religious Studies Department, I approached my dean and suggested that we should start a program that would help the University of Dayton do a better job hiring a diverse faculty that would support the university's mission.

The phrase "hiring for mission" leads to misunderstandings. Who does not hire for mission—*their* idea of the mission? Should anyone be fired for mission? Is hiring for mission something other than hiring good researchers and teachers? How intellectual is the Catholic mission? Does it apply primarily to hires in theology departments and campus ministry? Is it more relevant for certain parts of a university than others, for example, more for the humanities than the professions? Does it mean hiring pious people who are less than intellectually gifted? Can it be presumed that Catholic faculty, because of their Catholicism, see into reality more deeply than those who are not Catholic? Isn't it illegal to ask faculty candidates about their religious faith? If it were legal, would it even be relevant to ask a candidate about his or her personal faith? Does hiring for mission exclude hiring Jews, Muslims, agnostics, and atheists?

Is a "critical mass" of Catholics the same thing as 50 percent of the faculty being Catholic? Should we even be paying any attention to the percentage of Catholics on the faculty? Even if it were possible to hire only Catholics, should that be attempted? Is the commitment to diversity and pluralism just an effort to make a virtue out of necessity, that is, applauding diversity because that's the gender and ethnic profile the faculty now reflects? Should the aim be to create diversity in one institution, or between institutions? If Catholic universities followed the same hiring priorities as secular universities, would not their faculties look very similar to those at secular universities and end up eliminating an important form of diversity in higher education in the United States?

Such questions rise spontaneously when faculty discuss hiring for mission. At the University of Dayton, we decided that the best way for us to address this issue was to start from the "bottom up." We decided to begin to work directly with faculty, and especially with department chairs and heads of search committees—that is, with those who play key roles in the hiring process.

In anticipation of the many typical misunderstandings of what it means to hire for mission, we decided to set aside a generous amount of time for a small group of the faculty for confidential discussions. We organized off-campus overnight workshops that we held at a state park an hour's drive from campus. We put together a folder of readings, none very long, which dealt with the topics we wanted to discuss. The first evening session allowed for lengthy personal introductions, and then a discussion of several readings that situated Catholic higher education in the United States today; the next morning, we conducted two sessions, one on the typical misunderstandings of hiring for mission, and one that evaluated how well the university was doing, strengths and weaknesses, especially when it came to the intellectual work called for by its Catholic and Marianist mission. After lunch, we brainstormed practical initiatives ("best practices") in hiring for mission.

After several years, a consensus grew that hiring for mission had to be supplemented by more purposeful and continuous faculty development. The dean of the College of Arts and Sciences developed a second-year tenure track faculty retreat. By the spring of their second year, most faculty had settled sufficiently into their roles to understand more clearly the challenges and possibilities they had as teachers, researchers, and colleagues. What they still needed was a clearer understanding of the Catholic intellectual tradition applied to their teaching and research.

One reason these workshops worked is that highly respected lay faculty

who understood the university's mission led the entire workshop. They brief-
ly introduced each session, leaving ample time for discussion. They created an open and honest atmosphere. It was not uncommon for attendees to
admit that they were not looking forward to the workshop, but at its comple-
tion admitted that they had actually found it very helpful. They had expected "lectures" on Catholic identity rather than what they actually experienced:
thoughtful explorations of the complexities and importance of hiring for
mission.

Other Catholic universities and colleges have addressed this issue in still
other ways. Whatever the approach, if it does not result in hiring faculty who
can and wish to contribute to the mission of the university in ways appropriate to their disciplines, the distinctive character of Catholic higher education
runs the serious risk of disappearing over time.

In summary, hiring of faculty for mission needs to be faced squarely.
There are many wrong ways and some right ways to go about doing it. One of
the best ways is to engage the faculty themselves in that process. While hiring
for mission does not at all exclude non-Catholic faculty, it does focus on the
distinctive intellectual mission of a Catholic university—a focus that even
some Catholic faculty candidates may be unable or even unwilling to support.

Asking for Help: Faculty Formation

Besides being hired, faculty need to be socialized into the mission of the university. They need to see how their teaching and research relates to the university's mission. Developing curricula, general education programs, and special
majors and minors rooted in the mission of the university make it easier for
faculty to connect what they do with that mission. For example, general education programs built on themes of Christian anthropology, sacramentality,
faith and reason, not only draw on multiple disciplines, but make it easier for
faculty to relate to the mission intellectually. (It is often hardest to establish a
mission-related emphasis at the graduate level—unless, that is, sufficient resources and vision exist to make mission-related graduate programs a reality.)

Another way for presidents to influence the faculty is to endow chairs. The
faculty, however, should be involved in selecting the occupant. Moreover, the
chair should be located within a department, rather than report directly to the
president or provost. I also think that presidents should not establish free-
standing institutes designed to strengthen the mission. Such institutes make
it too easy for the rest of the faculty to ignore their responsibility for the

mission. Some faculty may dismiss faculty in endowed chairs appointed by administrators, and ignore special institutes, dismissing them as vehicles of the administration for pleasing donors, not places of serious scholarship.

However, if the leadership of the university puts serious intellectual work front and center, most of the faculty will respect such administrative initiatives. If the president is not perceived as a highly accomplished academic, the academic vice president should be. Presidents can't do it all. As Fr. Hesburgh's predecessor once told him, "You will do a lot better if you get off the horse and entice the best of the multitude to join you up front. Be sure that all those who help you achieve your vision receive a large share of the credit."

A vibrant intellectual community engaged in mission-focused research makes it easier for new faculty to see why hiring for mission is important. Other initiatives help faculty as well, such as released time for research. Less expensive ways to develop an intellectual community have also been used. For example, a reading group that meets over dinner every month, or during the summer, costs relatively little.

In 1990, when I served as provost at Dayton, I established a faculty-driven Forum on the Catholic Intellectual Tradition Today. With highly respected academic representatives from each division of the university, this commission received each year enough funds to organize conferences, invite speakers, make research grants, and keep the conversations on Catholic intellectual traditions alive. They supported faculty development in two ways: they themselves exemplified a commitment to Catholic intellectual tradition in a variety of disciplines and they invited other faculty to join them in that commitment.

A Catholic university benefits greatly when the strongest and most respected professors teach in the humanities, especially philosophy and theology. In the early 1990s, we established a Ph.D. program in theology. A highly respected group of theologians are now doing excellent research and teaching. Not every university can establish a Ph.D. program in theology, but no Catholic institution can afford to have weak departments of theology and philosophy.

Given all their other responsibilities, few presidents bring any of this about without a provost, deans, and faculty leaders who are committed to this same vision. Faculty with a rich sense of sacramentality find many ways to enhance the mission, be they in the professions, the social sciences, or the sciences.

Presidents and the Formation of Students

While it is encouraging that the BC/ACCU survey reports that most of the presidents of Catholic universities report a positive relationship with their local bishop as well as with their founding congregation, they also believed that their successors would not be as committed as they are to promoting the Catholic dimension.[14]

A president should not only lead an institution, but should also model personally what it means to be the leader of a Catholic university. Again, Fr. Hesburgh: "The greatest gift presidents can give their students is the example of their lives. Young adults are, whether they admit it or not, looking for public models of the kind of person they would like to become." If leaders in Catholic higher education can do better at selecting and forming faculty who support the mission, they will have taken a major step toward the appropriate formation of students.

That survey reported that less than a quarter of the students participated in retreats and liturgies—which is actually higher than the national average. There are, of course, many explanations as to why so few college students, especially men, participate in campus ministry programs. How much of the president's energy and budget should be devoted to strengthening campus ministry?[15]

What about Board Formation?

Board selection and formation are crucially important. An excellent president knows how to recruit a good board, and a good board knows how to select a good president. Robert M. Hutchins, the famous reforming president of the University of Chicago, once wrote that "any university needs a purpose, a vision of the end. The administrator must accept a special responsibility for the discussion, clarification, definition and proclamation of this end." That presidential responsibility requires that the board understand and support

---

[14] Cernera, *Lay Leaders in Catholic Higher Education*, p. 3.

[15] Especially in the second part of this essay, I have drawn freely on several of my own recent publications: "Academics and Campus Ministry: Two Different Worlds," in *Journal of Catholic Higher Education* 27, no. 2 (2008), pp. 1–15; "Distinctively Catholic: Keeping the Faith in Higher Education," in *Commonweal* (March 26 2010), pp. 9–13; and "Institutionalizing Catholic Identity," in *Journal of Catholic Higher Education* 31, no. 2 (2012), pp. 181–192. The last article was originally a presentation at the 8th International Conference on Catholic Social Thought and Management Education.

that vision. Most Catholic colleges and universities have created boards of trustees, dominantly lay, with real fiduciary responsibility for the mission and strategic direction of the university and the appointment or removal of the president. Often, they wield considerable financial clout. Their importance should be obvious.

But how well chosen and formed are our boards of trustees? For several years I was privileged to give 10 two-day workshops for boards of trustees at Catholic colleges and universities. In one part of the workshop, I asked them to list their responsibilities as board members. Not once did they list as among their responsibilities the following: protecting the independence of the university from external controls, defending the faculty's academic freedom, or evaluating annually their own performance. Most did not know how to articulate the intellectual dimensions of their institution. It has been the experience of many presidents that the graduates they appoint to their boards have little understanding of their role as board members, and more problematic, do not understand the nature of a university, or the distinctive academic Catholic character that their alma mater should have.

How does a president meet this challenge? First, it is important that the president ensure that at each board meeting an adequate amount of time is set aside for educating the board in the mission of the institution and its history and culture. Before each meeting, board members should assume that they will need to read texts that have to do with more than finances, investments, enrollment numbers, and building plans. Boards need to make sure that there are ways to thank and not reappoint members who are not actively involved.

While the president and the board chair usually play the key role in forming the agenda for the board meeting, they should not appear to "own" it, but rather solicit suggestions from the entire board, or at least the executive committee. Difficult questions should not be avoided. Presidents sometimes need confidential advice from board members; that advice will be valuable to the extent that board members understand the issues the president faces. Finally, good boards regularly evaluate not only the performance of the president, but also their own performance. Some very effective boards routinely ask at the end of their meetings whether they used their time together well and whether they stayed strategic and avoided the temptation to micromanage.

In a separate session before their first full board meeting, new board members should be informed of the board's norms, rules of engagement, and the behaviors of an effective board. It is also helpful if a recent major decision of the board that strengthened the core values of the institution is discussed. Informing the new board members of impending deliberations and decisions will allow them to be ready to participate in the first meeting. Some boards have asked a veteran board member to be a "mentor" for the new board member for the first year.[16]

If one of the most important roles of a board of trustees is the hiring of the president, then they also need to be adept at succession planning. Some religious orders have avoided doing this for as long as possible, hoping that they can continue to find among their diminishing numbers somebody they can appoint as president. University culture also makes it difficult to prepare faculty to become educational leaders. Faculty who want to enter administration are sometimes seen as "selling out" on their true academic vocation, or worse as going over to "the other side."

Vibrant educational institutions are always in the "recruiting" mode, looking for the best talent they can find, not just for members on the faculty, but even more so for academic leadership. Attentiveness to developing leadership facilitates choosing a new president. The board has already created a solid "bench" and will not be completely dependent on professional search firms.

Nationally, the Association of Catholic Colleges and Universities (ACCU), primarily a presidents' organization, holds its three-day annual convention in Washington, D.C. It would be an enlightening experience for presidents to bring some of their board members to these meetings, and to give a report on some of the most relevant presentations for discussion with their own board. Presidents often find the greatest value in talking confidentially with another president who faces similar problems. Presidents often live lonely lives. Confidants and mentors are important.

The ACCU features an online searchable database of "promising practices" for mission and identity issues, a handbook for mission officers and the *Journal of Catholic Higher Education,* which publishes articles on aspects of Catholic higher education. A recent issue covered how the Catholic intellectual tradition can be embodied in the curriculum of business schools.[17] Another journal, *Catholic Education: A Journal of Inquiry and Practice,* founded 15 years

---

[16] Some of the suggestions in this paragraph are drawn from an unpublished presentation by Steven Katsouros, S.J., of the University of San Francisco.

[17] See the *Journal of Catholic Higher Education* Summer 2012 issue.

ago, covers the entire span of Catholic education, from the primary to the university level.

The Relationship with the Founding Religious Community

Presidents need to be attentive to the charism of the founding religious order. A number of religious orders have worked on this. They draw out the educational implications of their spirituality. Faculty at some of these universities explore pedagogical ramifications of the order's charism. Even though Catholicism as a whole is deeper, older, and richer intellectually and spiritually than the charism of any religious order, presidents need to find ways, both old and new, to explore and communicate the charism, and do it in ways that strengthen the distinctive character of their universities.

The Collegium Program

Founded nearly 20 years ago, a second national organization, Collegium, joins young scholars finishing their doctorates and faculty early in their career with more experienced Catholic scholars for a full week of talks, discussion, and prayer, including a retreat day during which they have the opportunity to learn about the spiritual traditions of various religious orders. Collegium is designed to help young scholars understand the relationship of their faith to their intellectual life. It maintains a network among its graduates through a regular newsletter, online resources, reading lists, and fellowships for research opportunities. Thomas M. Landy, the founder and director of the program, edited *As Leaven in the World*, a collection of essays about the Catholic intellectual life.[18] Young scholars who attend this program are likely to be the future leaders of Catholic higher education. Few tasks are more neglected by presidents of Catholic universities than identifying and preparing the next generation of leaders for their institutions.

Conclusion

Now led by predominantly lay presidents and lay boards of trustees, staffed with highly credentialed faculty, fewer religious and more diverse students, and functioning in a more secular and commercialized culture, a "new era" in Catholic colleges and universities has arrived. Leaders of Catholic colleges and

---

[18] *As Leaven in the World: Catholic Perspectives on Faith, Vocation, and the Intellectual Life*, edited by Thomas Landy (Franklin, WI: Sheed & Ward, 2001).

universities need to work harder at developing the distinctive intellectual traditions of Catholicism. The challenges are both multiple and formidable.

One of the most important ways to meet these challenges is to hire and form faculty who respect and enhance that distinctive mission. Presidents are unable to do this by themselves; they need the collaboration of other administrators and the support of a board that knows what a Catholic university should be. That some Catholic universities have adopted practices and established programs that in fact strengthen their identity should be an encouragement for everyone who has been called and privileged to lead these special institutions.

Looking Forward: Catholic Higher Education in the 21st Century

WILLIAM P. LEAHY, S.J.

PRESIDENT, BOSTON COLLEGE

The essays in this volume provided context and focus for Boston College's October 2013 Sesquicentennial Symposium on four critical challenges facing Catholic higher education. Participants spoke from their personal experiences and diverse perspectives, adding greatly to the quality of discussions. They acknowledged that the widespread changes in American culture, higher education, and the Catholic community have dramatically affected Catholic higher education in the United States, particularly its mission and character, academic aspirations and quality, and financial viability. This final chapter highlights key comments and recommendations made during the symposium.

First, those present expressed appreciation for Fr. Michael Himes's understanding of the Catholic intellectual tradition, derived from his analysis and reflection on scriptural accounts of Creation and the Incarnation. Stressing the significance of God becoming man, he proposes that the more fully human individuals are, the more they can receive God. The Christian life calls for the greatest possible development of the human person, and becoming fully human is a religious act for those who believe that humanity is what they and God have in common.

Himes holds as an underlying principle of Catholic education that faculty members' pursuit of truth in their disciplines is effectively a search for what will make all people more human (and, from the Christian perspective, more like God). This conviction provides a starting point for a college or university community seeking to engage in a conversation about mission, no matter the members' backgrounds or religious beliefs. His advice: start with individuals' experiences, ask them to reflect on what gives meaning to their work and lives, and assume that deep down all people are wrestling with the most profound questions that can be asked about human life and the contemporary world. In his view, Catholic colleges and universities need to be more explicit about their distinctive character, presume curiosity in their campus communities about the Catholic tradition, and provide informal programs that draw faculty and administrators into reflecting on the common ground between their deepest commitments and the Catholic tradition.

Reflection and dialogue about the intersection of the Catholic faith and wider culture, of the ideal of "faith-seeking understanding," has been entrusted to universities since the 12th and 13th centuries. But today an insufficient number of academics, especially in Catholic institutions of higher education, understand the Catholic intellectual tradition, and even fewer are strongly committed to it. Given the current reality, Catholic schools need to identify, hire, and reward faculty willing and able to teach and write about ideas, values, and approaches shaped by Catholic life as well as by the Catholic theological and philosophical heritage. These faculty members should be invited into conversations on the meaning of human experience, integrating belief and intellect, and handing on faith today.

In addition, opportunities to learn about various dimensions of the Catholic intellectual tradition through conversation, workshops, and courses should be offered regularly by Catholic colleges and universities for campus members and for the wider community. Experts should be asked to research and publish monographs on contemporary issues from the perspectives of such Catholic theologians and philosophers as Augustine, Bonaventure, Aquinas, Newman, Maritain, and Rahner, and also encouraged to draw from the Catholic literary imagination.

Catholic schools with doctoral programs in history, theology, philosophy, and literature should ensure that Ph.D. students in those fields understand seminal Catholic intellectual figures so that these aspiring academics have some familiarity with aspects of the Catholic intellectual tradition and a disposition to convey knowledge and appreciation of it to their future students. Finally, individuals with the necessary skills and credibility must be encouraged to serve as advocates of viewpoints on curriculum, student life, and political and social issues reflective of Catholic sensibilities and convictions.

Symposium participants also engaged the complicated question of student formation. In his paper, Joseph A. Appleyard, S.J., traced the sweeping changes from colonial times to the early 20th century in student religious formation: changes in the curriculum and faculty involvement; and the increase of student affairs and campus ministry personnel. In most of American higher education, the result has been to turn the undergraduate years into a basically secular intellectual experience. To help remedy the current situation, Appleyard proposes a framework for reconceptualizing student formation in Catholic higher education based both on an incarnational perspective summarized in Michael Himes's insight that "what humanizes, divinizes," and on a research-based understanding of the psychological development of young adults.

Discussion participants agreed with Appleyard's analysis that Catholic colleges and universities faced four challenges in trying to inject the religious perspective into undergraduate life: (1) faculties' limited understanding of their role; (2) diverse faith backgrounds and expectations of students; (3) lack of experience and familiarity with student formation issues among student affairs personnel; and (4) the need for a philosophy of student formation for Catholic higher education.

To counter these difficulties, Catholic higher education must first articulate a compelling vision of student formation as an integral part of the undergraduate experience on Catholic campuses. The curriculum, especially core courses, should address not only subject matter and skills, but also how classes seek to help students reflect on what they believe and why, consider how they make important decisions, and how they can grow as people of integrity, sound judgment, and engaged citizens. To be true to their heritage, Catholic colleges and universities should enable their students to develop their gifts and be successful, but also increase their desire to serve others and be a leaven for good. Such student formation outcomes must be included in statements of institutional goals, and schools must recommit themselves to an integrated, collaborative approach to student formation and reestablish it as a priority for personnel in academic affairs, student life, and mission and ministry. Faculty especially must become reinvolved in student formation and view it as part of their commitment to teaching and service.

Furthermore, the parallel curriculum of powerful experiences—retreats, weekend programs, immersion opportunities, community service, and so on—must be made part of a coherent, strategic approach based on a sound theology of the person and drawing from the insights of developmental psychology. These aspects of student life simply cannot remain scattered and unrelated to the intellectual dimensions of college.

The third topic considered at the BC Symposium concerned the relationship of Catholic colleges and universities to the Church. In his essay on "'Catholic' as Descriptive of a University," Robert J. Kaslyn, S.J., J.C.D., notes that the link between a Catholic institution of higher education and the Church in the past was simple and cordially formal. Bishops and presidents were part of the leadership cohort in the Catholic community and operated from similar assumptions and norms. But conditions changed radically in the 1960s as Catholic schools expanded in size and scope, entered the academic mainstream of American higher education, and the number of religious in leadership positions and teaching ranks began to decline. In addition, criteria for hiring and promotion of faculty shifted to emphasize research and publication more than teaching and pastoral involvement, the curriculum lost the unifying influence of the neo-scholastic synthesis of philosophy and theology, and lay people became the majority on governing boards. As a result, many of the institutions' most visible signs of Catholicity became less obvious.

Subsequently, previous assumptions about what makes a college or university Catholic became a serious and pressing question for some in the Catholic community. In Kaslyn's view, the critical issue is maintaining communion with the Church, and he believes that Catholic colleges and universities today need to: (1) clarify the canonical status of an institution that describes itself as "Catholic"; (2) identify the competent ecclesiastical authority enabling use of "Catholic" as self-descriptive; (3) establish clearly the ownership of assets and liabilities; and (4) determine whether the use of the word "Catholic" is meant merely as a reference to historical foundation or describes a reality that permeates the entire mission and operation of the institution.

Discussion of Kaslyn's paper manifested little doubt that changes both in the Church and in American Catholic higher education since the late 1970s have led to sometimes neuralgic issues concerning the relationship of Catholic postsecondary institutions to the Church. But participants also maintained that the goal of communion with the Church has been furthered by extensive efforts of Catholic colleges and universities to reassert and promote their religious mission and heritage. Both the Church and schools share a common purpose and desire to maintain religious roots and commitments in an increasingly secular environment.

Those in attendance also recognized that canonical issues concerning separate incorporation and ownership of assets/liabilities must be resolved in a way that does not reverse the significant progress that American Catholic higher education has made because of the extraordinary commitment, expertise, and resources of lay trustees. Moreover, to foster healthy relationships, they recommended that leaders in Catholic colleges and universities maintain frequent and honest communication with local bishops, promote dialogue between the hierarchy and theologians, and offer assistance to the local Church by making institutional resources and personnel available to meet diocesan needs where possible.

Those at the symposium also discussed the broad issue of leadership in Catholic higher education, drawing from their own experience and the essay by James L. Heft, S.M., which summarized external and internal difficulties that have drawn the attention of Catholic college and university leaders in recent decades. They affirmed the vital role that presidential leadership must play in engaging and resolving critical challenges facing Catholic postsecondary schools, whether revitalizing the Catholic intellectual tradition, strengthening student formation efforts, addressing canonical matters, or identifying and recruiting students, administrators, faculty, and staff committed to the mission of Catholic higher education.

Catholic higher education must develop leaders who provide vision and decisions. A "vision" suggests a way of seeing and conceiving that is transformative, that offers realizable ideals so compelling that individuals are energized and willing to invest themselves in an enterprise far more effectively and extensively than they would have thought possible. Without vision and appropriate, timely decisions, institutions stagnate and drift, and people often settle for mediocrity. Issues must be engaged and conflicts resolved. John Ireland, archbishop of St. Paul in the late 19th and early 20th centuries, insisted that the timid move in crowds, but the brave in single file.

Presidents of Catholic colleges and universities should maintain and enhance the religious heritage and distinctive character of their institutions, so critical to enrollment, fund-raising, and relationships with bishops and the larger Catholic community. They have to take the lead in promoting a dialogue with traditions that shaped and continue to shape their institutions, and then adapt this heritage to changed and changing circumstances. Leaders of Catholic colleges and universities must also safeguard the integrity of their schools, especially when external forces seek to infringe on faculty rights or institutional autonomy.

Heads of Catholic higher educational institutions and the Association of Catholic Colleges and Universities must take steps to prepare succeeding generations of leaders at all levels. Younger administrators and faculty have to be persuaded to consider educational leadership as a vocation and a form of ministry, and these individuals must be provided opportunities to develop needed academic credentials, administrative experience, and familiarity with the mission and heritage of Catholic schools. Without such interventions, there will not be qualified candidates for leadership vacancies, especially presidencies, and that void will cause immense harm to the Catholic character and commitments of schools.

Catholic colleges and universities today have changed greatly since 1960. They have improved significantly in students, faculty, facilities, and academic quality, particularly on the undergraduate level. Efforts to raise institutional profiles and to obtain funds from a variety of benefactors have shown impressive results. They have benefited in critical ways from committed, generous trustees. But enabling Catholic higher education to remain true to its intellectual, social, and religious heritage and to influence American academic culture and wider society in the coming decades will require intelligence, courage, tenacity, and hope. In particular, the challenges discussed at the symposium concerning the Catholic intellectual tradition, student formation, relations with the Church, and leadership development must be taken seriously and resolved successfully. For that task, the prophet Jeremiah offers words of comfort and inspiration: "For I know the plans I have for you, says the Lord, plans for welfare and not for evil, to give you a future and hope...when you seek me with all your heart, I will be found by you" (29: 11,13).

Survey of Catholic College Presidents

JESSICA A. GREENE

DIRECTOR, OFFICE OF INSTITUTIONAL RESEARCH, BOSTON COLLEGE

T he purpose of "Critical Issues in Catholic Higher Education: Presidents' Survey" was to explore the attitudes and beliefs of presidents of Catholic colleges and universities about four key issues facing Catholic higher education in the coming decades:

1. institutional leadership;

2. student religious formation;

3. the Catholic intellectual tradition; and

4. the institution's relationship with the hierarchical Church.

During the late fall of 2012, Boston College administered the Critical Issues survey to all Catholic college and university presidents in the United States, based upon data supplied by the Association of Catholic Colleges and Universities, the cosponsor of the project. Of the 194 presidents surveyed, 119 (62 percent) responded.[1]

---

[1]   In order to assess the representativeness of the survey's participating institutions, data from a series of variables were compared between the population (i.e., the national set of Catholic colleges and universities, n=194) to the sample (i.e., the set of responding institutions, n=119). Across a variety of metrics, all sourced from the Integrated Postsecondary Education Data System, the federal government's core higher-education data collection program, sample characteristics were on par with those of the population, and the comparability of results thus serves to validate the dataset and support its generalizability to the larger community of Catholic higher-education institutions (please reference the supplement to Appendix A for comparison data and a list of participating institutions).

Survey Highlights

- Over half (57 percent) of the presidents who responded are lay people and of these lay presidents, only about one-quarter (28 percent) are the first lay person to have served in this role at their current institution.

- Investment is being made in programs that address leadership specifically at Catholic institutions (80 percent of institutions offer programs of this type for administrators and faculty), and yet the lack of administrators and faculty who can serve as leaders who promote the institution's Catholic mission and character was frequently cited by presidents as a challenge and concern.

- The majority of presidents (54 percent) noted that less than 25 percent of their undergraduate student population participates in religious retreat programs.

- While eight out of 10 presidents (82 percent) commented that the Catholic intellectual tradition somewhat or greatly influences teaching on their campus, only half (49 percent) noted the same level of influence with regard to research activities.

- Half of the presidents described the relationship with their bishop as close, with four out of 10 communicating five or more times per year with their bishop.

FOCUS AREA I: Leadership

The participants were asked to comment on their overall familiarity with the Catholic dimensions of their institution's mission both prior to and since their appointment as president. They were also asked about any leadership development they engaged in through programs specific to Catholic institutions and to what degree they, and their trustees, faculty, and administrator counterparts, devote time and effort to the support of the institution's Catholic dimensions.

While about half (56 percent) of lay presidents responded that they were very familiar with the Catholic dimensions of their institution's mission before serving as president, 80 percent of religious presidents did so ("religious presidents" include any president who has a religious status such as Sister or Jesuit). Only 16 percent of lay presidents indicated that they have ever enrolled in theology graduate course work versus 82 percent of religious presidents. While religious presidents' participation in programs that focused on leadership development in Catholic institutions did outpace that of lay presidents, differences between the two groups were less pronounced (78 percent versus 68 percent, respectively). Of the presidents who were 60 years old or younger (44 percent of the sample), 70 percent noted that they were familiar with the Catholic dimensions of their institution's mission versus 63 percent of the older presidents. Eight out of 10 younger presidents have participated in Catholic-focused leadership development programs versus 66 percent of the older group.

While more lay presidents reported spending at least 30 percent of their time annually promoting their mission's Catholic dimensions than did religious presidents, they were less confident that these efforts would result in an eventual successor who would also work to promote these aspects. Female presidents reported spending more time promoting the Catholic dimensions of their institution's mission, yet were less confident that it will be sustained with future leadership.

GRAPHS 1 + 2: Time spent promoting Catholic dimensions of institution's mission (% reporting more than 30%) and degree of confidence successor will promote Catholic dimensions of institution's mission (% reporting confident and very confident)

GRAPH 1: Lay & Religious Presidents

GRAPH 2: Female & Male Presidents

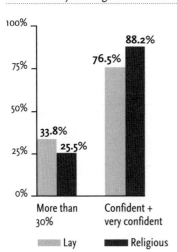

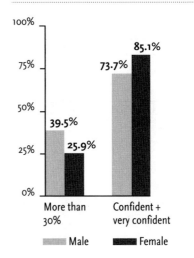

Presidents were asked to report on the degree to which trustees, faculty, and administrators understood the Catholic dimensions of the institution's mission, along with their involvement with it and their effectiveness in promoting it. Across all three areas (i.e., understanding, involvement, and effectiveness in promoting), administrators outscored both trustees and faculty. The scores for each group declined from the first area to the third— that is, while each group had a considerable understanding of the Catholic dimensions, their involvement scores were lower and their ability to effectively promote these Catholic dimensions was the lowest (in the "somewhat effective" category).

GRAPH 3:   To what extent do trustees, faculty, and administrators understand, are involved with, and are effective in promoting the Catholic dimensions of your institution's mission?

Scale: 1 = Minimal to 4 = Very

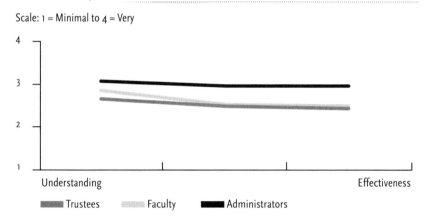

Finally, as a means to expand upon their responses, presidents were offered the opportunity to describe two challenges that will affect the leadership of Catholic higher education in the coming decades. While the range of comments was extensive and spanned such topics as the public's perception of the Church, the impact of political polarization, and the diminishing number of priests and religious, the primary challenge presented by responding presidents focused on staffing for mission and the consequent dynamic between changing leadership demographics and the ability to remain a mission-oriented institution, where mission is grounded specifically in the institution's Catholic foundation.

The challenge of staffing for mission included issues associated with finding staff who are both qualified for leadership positions and able to articulate Catholic values in support of the mission of a Catholic college or university. Presidents noted:

- [the need for] individuals with some theological background prepared to assume leadership.
- [the] difficulty in [the] recruitment of committed Catholic faculty into leadership.
- [the] challenge of hiring for mission throughout the university.
- the preparation of future leaders who place a high priority on leadership in Catholic higher education in their capacity as campus administrators and senior faculty.
- [there is] much greater difficulty in finding/hiring those with a substantive background in Catholic theology.

Church leadership was the presidents' second most frequently cited challenge. Their comments ranged from those that reflected the nature of relationships between the institution and the local bishop to the perceived alienation of lay Catholics from the Church hierarchy. Their specific concerns included:

- [there will be a] reduced pool of qualified and interested leaders if the hierarchy continues to emphasize a narrow critical agenda.
- a challenge is the model of a shared academic governance in the context of a hierarchical Church.
- [the] ossification of the hierarchy intellectually (already well advanced, but worse is yet to come).
- bishops seem to lack understanding about the needs of higher education.
- [there is a] fractious relationship between the Church and members.
- [there are] hierarchical expectations without support.
- the positions of the hierarchy will deter good candidates.
- [a challenge is] the tension between the institutional Church and the mission of Catholic higher education.

While fewer of the presidents articulated financial concerns, and their bearing on leadership, many did remark on the need for "financial resources to strengthen and attract the best faculty and administration" and noted that generalized financial pressures, which affect all types of institutions, cannot be discounted, particularly in terms of "finding leaders who are willing to lead during difficult financial times."

FOCUS AREA II: Student Formation

A second area the presidents were asked to comment on was that of student formation, conceptualized to mean an explicit and intentional approach to helping students move toward more critically aware forms of knowing, choosing, and living authentically.

While the majority of presidents (85 percent) noted that their campuses do have an office specifically charged with promoting the Catholic dimensions of their institution through student formation programs, participation in these programs, particularly those with a religious orientation, was variable. That is, while religious presidents noted more frequent participation rates in religious activities by their undergraduate students than did their lay president counter-parts, both religious and lay presidents cited infrequent participation in these types of programs for the majority (60 percent) of their graduate student pop-ulation. Similarly, over half of both lay and religious presidents noted that less than 25 percent of their undergraduate and graduate student communities participate in religious retreat programs.

Interestingly, as the percentage of freshmen receiving Pell grants increases, the frequency of participation in both religious activities or retreats decreases (Pell grants, federally funded grants awarded to students with significant financial aid needs that do not have to be repaid, are often considered an indicator of the socioeconomic status of a student population). As an institu-tion's endowment increases, so too does the frequency of participation in religious activities and retreats. These findings correspond to presidents' comments that "more students will face financial challenges [and] will work more" and their having to work "more and more hours while carrying a full course load, will thereby limit their involvement," not only in student forma-tion programs but in all types of opportunities that help to shape the undergraduate experience.

GRAPH 4: Responses by Lay and Religious Presidents Regarding Undergraduate Student Participation in Religious Activities

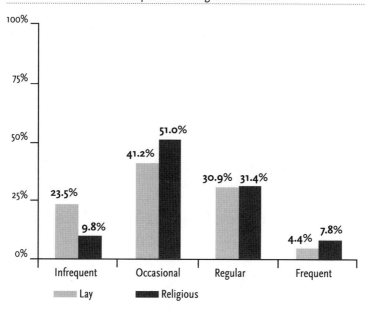

GRAPH 5: Responses by Lay and Religious Presidents Regarding Graduate Student Participation in Religious Activities

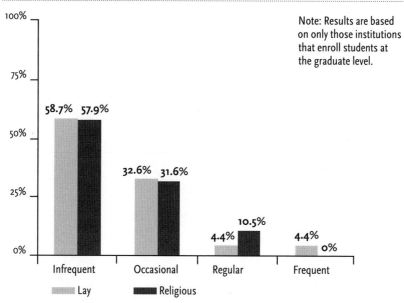

Note: Results are based on only those institutions that enroll students at the graduate level.

As with the topic of leadership, presidents were asked to report on the degree to which trustees, faculty, and administrators understand the role of student formation and how effective they are in promoting student formation at their institutions. Similar to the results for Catholic dimensions and mission, each group declined from the first area to the third—that is, while each group had a moderate understanding of student formation, faculty and administrators were somewhat effective in promoting student formation and trustees only minimally effective.

GRAPH 6: To what extent do trustees, faculty, and administrators understand, and how effective are they in promoting, the Catholic dimensions of your institution's mission?

Scale: 1 = Minimal to 4 = Very

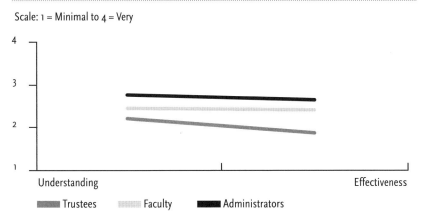

The presidents were invited to submit two challenges they considered important in their effect on student formation in the coming decades. "Inadequate pre-formation" and the shift in student demographics were the most common comments offered.

"Inadequate pre-formation," the lack of prior Catholic formative education and experiences, approaches a state some described as "religious illiteracy." The prevalence of this "increasingly un-churched student population" concerns presidents since many of the current student formation models in place at their universities are grounded on faith formation opportunities that assume a foundation. The minimal religious background and preparation their students exhibit suggests a reengineering of these programs, which some presidents are reluctant to address—the perceived risk being that to move too far away from faith-oriented programs conflicts directly with the institution's mission and purpose for being. As described by presidents:

- [there is] mostly an "un-churched" generation entering college.
- traditional students seem less knowledgeable about the Catholic faith.
- [there is a] growing population of Catholic students who lack understanding of the Catholic tradition.
- [there is a] lack of adequate catechesis in childhood, adolescence.
- precollege religious education [has been] dismal for the last 40 years in the Catholic Church.

Presidents also anticipate that continued student demographic shifts will challenge student formation efforts, since many institutions are currently experiencing a transition in their student population to one that includes fewer Catholics and greater numbers of minority and/or first-generation students. Collectively, the presidents noted that the "declining percent of Catholic students in [the] total population" and affiliated "increase in the diversity of faith traditions" present difficulties in "cultivating student formation since the diverse student body demands a more specialized approach." Many presidents noted that their resources would be insufficient to enable an expansion of student formation programming that could address the array of student groups. Presidents also noted that, for their Catholic students, there is an increasingly apparent disconnect between students' and the institutional Church's views on social issues; this wedge, with the potential to alienate, offers yet another challenge to student formation.

As with the topic of leadership, presidents commenting on the challenges of student formation also frequently mentioned funding and cost considerations. As they struggle in the face of multiple demands to most appropriately allocate financial and human resources to student formation programs, many also cited the additional pressure from the public, media, and elected officials who understand higher education as "job preparation."

Finally, a handful of comments pointed to the more looming topical area of "cultural indifference." Explaining that today's world is so fast-paced and distraction-laden, some presidents observed that the core activities of student formation simply cannot compete. As articulated by one president: "The desire for instant connection makes reflection, retreat, and introspection seem foreign to too many today. Formation is about reflection, relationships, and commitment." Another president explained that today's world does not afford students "the time needed to focus on how to live a life."

FOCUS AREA III: The Catholic Intellectual Tradition

Presidents were asked to rate the degree to which campus constituents understand the Catholic intellectual tradition, conceived to be the continually evolving heritage of faith that seeks understanding, as well as how effective they are in its promotion. Presidents gave low ratings to their administrators, faculty, and trustees' understanding and effectiveness, yet the majority responded that the Catholic intellectual tradition substantially influences both teaching and research at their institutions. Slightly less than one-quarter (21 percent) of presidents noted that *Ex Corde Ecclesiae* had a significant impact on the Catholic dimensions of their college or university. No substantive differences emerged based on the demographics of the president (e.g., their religious status or age). On average, institutions require seven undergraduate credits in theology or religious studies.

GRAPH 7: To what extent do trustees, faculty, and administrators understand, and how effective are they in promoting, the Catholic intellectual tradition?

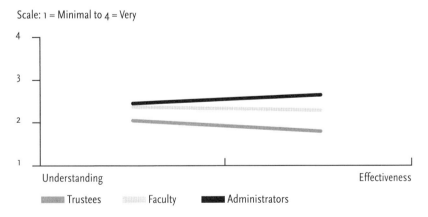

Scale: 1 = Minimal to 4 = Very

Note: Despite these low ratings, eight out of 10 presidents noted that the Catholic intellectual tradition influences teaching *somewhat* or a *great deal* at their institution. Half of all responding presidents noted that the Catholic intellectual tradition influences research *somewhat* or a *great deal* at their institution.

When asked to comment on challenges, the overwhelming majority of presidents cited "faculty" as the primary complication to the work of revitalizing the Catholic intellectual tradition. They remarked that "faculty [are] not personally committed," have a complete "lack of understanding [of] and preparation" in the Catholic intellectual tradition, and, perhaps most disconcerting, lack any interest in pursuing a knowledge of the Catholic intellectual tradition to such an extent that it was described by some as "faculty resistance." A related issue cited was the impending retirements of many current faculty who do "embrace, and are well versed, in the Catholic intellectual tradition" and the difficulty of "finding and attracting well-qualified Catholic faculty" and then subsequently "hiring and then engaging these new/young faculty with little or no formal exposure to the Catholic intellectual tradition." One president asked: "Who will be effective articulators of the Tradition?"

Many presidents theorized that faculty members' indifference to the Catholic intellectual tradition stemmed from their "perception of Church as a censor" and "wariness" about the idea of "living for mission." Others noted that there is simply a lack of communication and understanding of the topic, one explaining that "intellectual specialization narrows hiring choices (e.g., many of our computer scientists are neither Christian nor American") and that the reality of a diverse faculty corps emphasizes the need for enhanced dialogue. Many comments suggested a lack of clarity with regard to who is ultimately responsible for the sustenance and promotion of an institution's Catholic intellectual tradition. As summarized by one president, "When Catholic religious are serving in key leadership roles, the other members of the campus community have an expectation that those leaders are primarily responsible for the message of the Catholic intellectual tradition, etc., rather than shared ownership."

FOCUS AREA IV: Relationship with the Church

Finally, presidents were asked to describe their institution's relationship with the Catholic Church. Many presidents cited a positive relationship with both their local bishop and founding or sponsoring religious community, with 50 percent describing the relationship with their local bishop and 84 percent describing the relationship with their founding or sponsoring religious community as close. Roughly half (56 percent) of presidents noted their bishop takes a "great deal" of interest in how their institutions fulfill the Catholic dimensions of their mission. While the frequency of communication between presidents and bishops varied, 60 percent of presidents noted that they communicate with their local bishop at least three to four times a year and 40 percent correspond with their bishop five or more times a year.

Even with the varied levels of communication between presidents and bishops, 75 percent of presidents described the canonical status of their institution as very clear with a general understanding as to the ownership of physical assets and the appropriate role of the bishop. With regard to the topics addressed between presidents and bishops, a little over two-thirds of presidents (68 percent) noted that bishops did not typically express concern over campus programs or community members, although one-quarter did affirm that the bishop had privately expressed concern about individuals or programs they deemed inappropriate for a Catholic campus.

Asked to identify challenges that might affect their institution's relationship with their bishop and/or founding religious community, presidents identified bishop turnover (and the uncertainty associated with transitioning to a new bishop) and the declining number of religious as most affecting their relationship with the Church. Presidents offered personal accounts of these challenges:

- In my 10 years, we have had three archbishops. Each has had varying interest in our Catholic university.
- Due to the impending change of the local bishop, a new relationship will need to be established with the new bishop.
- At present I have no relationship; it all depends on who your bishop is.
- [There is] unpredictability of leadership—we are between bishops.
- [A new bishop] could have an understanding of the Catholic intellectual tradition and not nurture that tradition with his authority.
- Our founding community will not exist in 10 years.
- For our founding community, [how will we] root the charism and the institution as membership declines?
- How can we maintain an active role for the sponsoring community as their numbers decline and their presence becomes less visible?
- The declining number of Jesuits sets up challenges re: what the meaning of sponsorship actually entails.
- A hierarchy that has a limited understanding of higher-education culture.

In addition to comments reflecting their institution's direct relation to their bishop and/or their founding community, some presidents also mentioned challenges coming from the broader Church. Many noted, for example, "the increasing conservative movement in the institutional Church" and the problems trying to maintain academic freedom in the face of the challenges of "speakers with views contrary to Church teachings" and the "issues of contemporary society and social norms versus Catholic doctrine."

As a final point, it is very important to note that while many presidents cited the challenges, several described relationships with their bishop and founding community that have been built on mutual respect and affection and a shared understanding of mission. Many described these relationships as "strong, positive, and collaborative" and "very supportive."

Summary

In order to afford presidents the opportunity to comment on areas of particular interest to themselves and their institutions, they were asked to identify their greatest concerns and hopes for the future of Catholic higher education. Presidents concluded the survey with a range of remarks, but the majority reflected topics previously introduced, such as staffing for mission, meeting the needs of diverse student populations, engaging faculty in the Catholic intellectual tradition, and enhancing relationships with the institution's local bishop and the broader Church. The presidents' reiteration of these topics in their final statements reinforces the weight they place on these areas and suggests they are worthy of additional review and discussion.

Compelling was the presidents' identification of student outcomes as a source for both concern and hope. Recognizing the tremendous value of Catholic higher education, they hoped that Catholic institutions will continue to produce graduates who are "ethical" and "just" and who serve as "tomorrow's thoughtful and compassionate young people" dedicated to civic engagement and "society's welfare." The companion concern they cited, however, is the difficulty they seem to have in communicating their institution's ability "to prepare future leaders who will bring good...into the public square."

Ultimately, the synthesis of the presidents' comments showed that they believed the solidification of Catholic identity is critical to the future of Catholic higher education. They are concerned that the challenges of today may "result in institutions straying from [their] Catholic identity rather than embracing it" and that "the identity and mission of [an] institution is often compromised or unable to function as the marketplace becomes increasingly complicated and competitive." The fear of "remaining Catholic only in name" was expressed and many presidents noted that "secularization" is a force that seriously undercuts the "relevance" of our nation's Catholic colleges and universities. In the midst of these concerns, however, many presidents emphasized that collaborative work between religious and lay leaders is helping to navigate the challenges. Many presidents remain hopeful that they can continue to accomplish one of Catholic higher education's primary goals, that "the very students we are graduating will become our greatest leaders in Church and society."

Comparison of Population and Sample Characteristics

In order to assess the representativeness of the survey's participating institutions, data from a series of variables were compared between the population (i.e., the national set of Catholic colleges and universities, n=194) and the sample (i.e., the set of responding institutions, n=119).

Across a variety of metrics, sample characteristics were on par with those of the population, and the comparability of results thus serves to validate the dataset and support its generalizability to the larger community of Catholic higher education institutions. For example, in the population, 58.7 percent of the institutions were within the Carnegie Classification category of "Master's Colleges and Universities," which corresponds well to the sample statistic of 58.1 percent.

An exception to these overall results was in the category of endowment, where the mean value for the population was $121 million yet for responding institutions the mean value for fiscal year 2011 endowment levels was at $159 million.

Note: The source for both population and sample characteristics data is the Integrated Postsecondary Education Data System (IPEDS), the federal government's core higher education data collection program. Since IPEDS requires time to compile and test collected data, there is typically a lag between when individual institutions submit their data and its subsequent availability to the public. Thus, academic and fiscal year data for 2011 are presented in the below table for the majority of variables.

Institutions by Characteristics

	Population	Sample

CARNEGIE CLASSIFICATION

	Population	Sample
Associate's Colleges	4.8%	4.3%
Baccalaureate Colleges	21.7%	20.5%
Doctorate-Granting Universities	12.2%	14.5%
Master's Colleges and Universities	58.7%	58.1%
Special Focus Institutions: Theological Seminaries	0.5%	0.9%
Special Focus Institutions: Health Professions Schools *(other)*	2.1%	1.7%

REGION

	Population	Sample
Mid-Atlantic	18.0%	16.0%
Midwest	35.1%	37.0%
Northeast	25.3%	26.9%
South	8.8%	10.1%
Southwest	4.6%	4.2%
West	8.2%	5.9%

TUITION AND FEES 2011–2012

	Population	Sample
Average annual tuition	$26,481	$26,987
Institutions with annual tuition <= $15,000	7.9%	6.8%
Institutions with annual tuition between $15,001–$25,000	31.7%	32.5%
Institutions with annual tuition between $25,001–$35,000	49.7%	47.9%
Institutions with annual tuition between $35,001–$45,000	10.6%	12.8%

ENDOWMENT ASSETS FISCAL YEAR 2011

	Population	Sample
Average endowment as of fiscal year 2011	$121,202,937	$158,728,439
Institutions with FY11 endowment of <= $1,000,000	1.6%	2.6%
Institutions with FY11 endowment between $1,000,001–$9,999,999	22.4%	21.9%
Institutions with FY11 endowment between $10,000,000–$19,999,999	16.4%	15.8%
Institutions with FY11 endowment between $20,000,000–$39,999,999	22.4%	22.8%
Institutions with FY11 endowment between $40,000,000–$99,999,999	15.3%	10.5%
Institutions with FY11 endowment between $100,000,000–$249,999,999	12.0%	14.0%
Institutions with FY11 endowment >= $250,000,000	9.8%	12.3%

Institutions by Characteristics

	Population	Sample

ACCEPTANCE RATE FALL 2011

Average acceptance rate for freshmen entering in fall 2011	66.1%	65.0%
Institutions with an acceptance rate of <= 50%	14.5%	17.7%
Institutions with an acceptance rate between 51%–65%	30.7%	31.9%
Institutions with an acceptance rate between 66%–80%	38.0%	33.6%
Institutions with an acceptance rate between 81%–100%	16.8%	16.8%

ADMISSIONS YIELD FALL 2011

Average yield rate for freshmen entering in fall 2011	29.6%	28.9%
Institutions with a yield rate of <= 20%	26.3%	30.1%
Institutions with a yield rate between 21%–30%	34.1%	33.6%
Institutions with a yield rate between 31%–40%	22.9%	21.2%
Institutions with a yield rate between 41%–50%	10.6%	8.8%
Institutions with a yield rate between 51%–100%	6.1%	6.2%

ENROLLED FRESHMEN FALL 2011

Average freshmen class size for fall 2011	522	584
Institutions with an entering freshmen class of <= 200	23.4%	22.1%
Institutions with an entering freshmen class between 201–500	38.6%	35.4%
Institutions with an entering freshmen class between 501–1,000	26.1%	26.5%
Institutions with an entering freshmen class between 1,001–3,000	12.0%	15.9%

PERCENT OF FRESHMEN RECEIVING PELL GRANTS 2010–2011

On average % of freshmen receiving Pell grants	40.5%	38.9%
Institutions with <= 20% of freshmen receiving Pell grants	11.6%	14.5%
Institutions with between 21%–30% of freshmen receiving Pell grants	16.9%	16.2%
Institutions with between 31%–40% of freshmen receiving Pell grants	27.5%	25.6%
Institutions with between 41%–50% of freshmen receiving Pell grants	16.4%	18.8%
Institutions with between 51%–60% of freshmen receiving Pell grants	17.5%	18.8%
Institutions with between 61%–100% of freshmen receiving Pell grants	10.1%	6.0%

Institutions by Characteristics   Population Sample

TOTAL STUDENT HEADCOUNT FALL 2011

	Population	Sample
Average student headcount	3,840	4,282
Institutions with a headcount <= 1,000 students	10.6%	11.1%
Institutions with a headcount between 1,001–2,500 students	35.4%	34.2%
Institutions with a headcount between 2,501–5,000 students	32.8%	30.8%
Institutions with a headcount between 5,001–10,000 students	14.3%	13.7%
Institutions with a headcount >= 10,001 students	6.9%	10.3%

GRADUATION RATE 2011 (2005 cohort completing in 150% of normal time)

	Population	Sample
Average 2011 graduation rate	56.8%	58.0%
Institutions with a 2011 graduation rate of <= 40%	15.0%	17.2%
Institutions with a 2011 graduation rate between 41%–60%	42.2%	37.1%
Institutions with a 2011 graduation rate between 61%–80%	34.2%	31.9%
Institutions with a 2011 graduation rate between 81%–100%	8.6%	13.8%

TOTAL FTE FACULTY/STAFF FALL 2011

	Population	Sample
Average total FTE faculty/staff	627.2	712.6
Institutions with an FTE faculty/staff of <= 200	18.0%	18.8%
Institutions with an FTE faculty/staff between 201–500	47.6%	46.2%
Institutions with an FTE faculty/staff between 501–1,000	18.5%	15.4%
Institutions with an FTE faculty/staff between 1,001–2,000	10.1%	10.3%
Institutions with an FTE faculty/staff between 2,001–5,500	5.8%	9.4%

Participating Institutions

Albertus Magnus College

Alvernia University

Anna Maria College

Aquinas College

Assumption College

Assumption College for Sisters

Ave Maria University

Avila University

Barry University

Bellarmine University

Benedictine College

Benedictine University

Boston College

Brescia University

Caldwell College

Calumet College of Saint Joseph

Cardinal Stritch University

Carlow University

Catholic Distance University

Chaminade University of Honolulu

Christian Brothers University

Clarke University

College of Mount Saint Vincent

College of Saint Benedict

College of Saint Mary

College of the Holy Cross

Creighton University

DePaul University

DeSales University

Divine Word College

Dominican University

Donnelly College

Duquesne University of the Holy Spirit

Edgewood College

Elms College

Fairfield University

Felician College

Fontbonne University

Fordham University

Gannon University

Georgetown University

Georgian Court University

Gonzaga University

Gwynedd Mercy College

Hilbert College

Holy Cross College

Holy Family University

John Carroll University

Labouré College

Le Moyne College

Lewis University

Loras College

Loyola University Chicago

Loyola University Maryland

Madonna University

Marian Court College

Marian University

Marquette University

Marymount College

Mercyhurst University

Mexican American Catholic College

Mount Mercy University

Mount Saint Mary College

Mount Saint Mary's University

Neumann University

Newman University

Notre Dame College

Ohio Dominican University

Our Lady of Holy Cross College

Our Lady of the Lake College

Our Lady of the Lake University

Presentation College

Providence College

Quincy University

Regis College

Regis University

Rivier University

Rockhurst University

Rosemont College of the
    Holy Child Jesus

Sacred Heart University

Saint Ambrose University

Saint Bonaventure University

Saint Catharine College

Saint Francis University

Saint Gregory's University

Saint John's University (Minnesota)

Saint John's University (New York)

Saint Joseph's College

Saint Leo University

Saint Mary of the Woods College

Saint Mary's College of CA

Saint Michael's College

Saint Thomas Aquinas College

Saint Thomas University

Salve Regina University

Santa Clara University

Seton Hall University

Seton Hill University

Siena Heights University

Spring Hill College Institution

Stonehill College

The College of New Rochelle

Trocaire College

University of Dayton

University of Detroit Mercy

University of Notre Dame

University of Portland

University of Saint Francis

University of Saint Joseph

University of Saint Mary

University of San Francisco

University of Scranton

University of St. Francis

University of the Incarnate Word

Villanova University

Viterbo University

Walsh University

Wheeling Jesuit University

Xavier University

Participants in the Boston College Sesquicentennial Symposium on Catholic Higher Education

Presents in Attendance

Philip Boroughs, S.J.
President, College of the Holy Cross

Margaret Carney, O.S.F.
President, St. Bonaventure University

Daniel Curran
President, University of Dayton

John J. DeGioia
President, Georgetown University

Peter M. Donohue, O.S.A.
President, Villanova University

Janet Eisner, S.N.D.
President, Emmanuel College

Michael E. Engh, S.J.
President, Santa Clara University

Michael Galligan-Stierle
President and Chief Executive Officer, Association of Catholic Colleges and Universities

Michael J. Garanzini, S.J.
President, Loyola University Chicago

John H. Garvey
President, Catholic University

Dennis H. Holtschneider, C.M.
President, DePaul University

William P. Leahy, S.J.
President, Boston College

Andrea J. Lee, I.H.M.
President, St. Catherine University

Brian J. Shanley, O.P.
President, Providence College

Michael J. Sheeran, S.J.
President, Association of Jesuit Colleges and Universities

Authors of Background Papers

J. A. Appleyard, S.J.
Professor Emeritus, Boston College

Jessica A. Greene
Director, Office of Institutional Research, Boston College

James L. Heft, S.M.
Alton M. Brooks Professor of Religion, University of Southern California

Michael J. Himes
Professor, Theology Department, Boston College

Robert J. Kaslyn, S.J.
Dean of the School of Canon Law, The Catholic University of America

David J. O'Brien
Loyola Professor Emeritus, College of the Holy Cross

Other Boston College Participants

William Bole
Office of Marketing Communications

Terrence P. Devino, S.J.
Vice President and University Secretary

Robert R. Newton
Special Assistant to the President

Contributors

JOSEPH A. APPLEYARD, S.J., is professor emeritus at Boston College. Most recently he served as the executive assistant to the provincial of the New England Province of the Society of Jesus. Fr. Appleyard graduated from Boston College in 1953 and holds a doctorate in English from Harvard University as well as degrees in philosophy from Weston College and theology from the Canisianum in the Netherlands. Fr. Appleyard became a member of Boston College's English department in 1967. In his 43 years of service to the University he served as department chairperson, rector of the Jesuit Community, and Boston College's first vice president for University Mission and Ministry.

JESSICA A. GREENE, the director of Institutional Research at Boston College, has spent her career in research administration, first in market research in the private sector and then transitioning to educational research in her first position at Boston College in 1997 as a data manager. She earned her bachelor's degree in economics from the College of the Holy Cross, her master's from the University of Southern California, and her Ph.D. in educational research, measurement, and evaluation from Boston College. Her publications have centered on urban Catholic schools, survey design, assessment, and data warehousing.

JAMES L. HEFT, S.M., is the Alton Brooks Professor of Religion and the founder and president of the Institute of Advanced Catholic Studies at the University of Southern California. After receiving his doctorate in historical theology from the University of Toronto, he served the University of Dayton in many roles, teaching historical, systematic, and moral theology, and acting as chancellor and provost. Fr. Heft has served on and chaired the board of the American Association of Catholic Colleges and Universities, and was the recipient of the Theodore Hesburgh Award for distinguished service to Catholic Higher Education in 2011.

MICHAEL J. HIMES is a priest of the Roman Catholic Diocese of Brooklyn and a professor of theology at Boston College. A renowned contributor to Catholic thought, Fr. Himes received his B.A. from Cathedral College, his M.Div. from the Seminary of the Immaculate Conception, and his Ph.D. from the University of Chicago. A prolific writer and lecturer who has often been honored for his dedication to students, he is not only an active contributor to academic discussions around the questions of systematic theology, but he has also published more popular works, including *The Mystery of Faith: An Introduction to Catholicism*, which is used in RCIA programs across the country.

ROBERT J. KASLYN, S.J., a Jesuit from the New York Province, serves as the dean of the School of Canon Law at The Catholic University of America. He holds an S.T.B. and S.T.L. from Regis College, University of Toronto, and a doctorate in canon law from Saint Paul University in Ottawa. Fr. Kaslyn's special interests are ecclesiology and the Sacrament of Orders. He is widely published, including the book *"Communion with the Church" and the Code of Canon Law* and articles in *The Jurist, Studia Canonica,* and *Roman Replies and Advisory Opinions.* He has taught at the Weston School of Theology in Cambridge, Massachusetts, and served as a judge of the Diocesan Tribunal in Worcester, Massachusetts. In addition to his role as dean, he is also involved in canonical advocacy, advising institutions, civil law firms, and individuals on various issues.

WILLIAM P. LEAHY, S.J., a member of the Wisconsin Province of the Society of Jesus, became the 25th president of Boston College in July 1996. He came to Boston College from Marquette University, where he served 11 years as a faculty member and administrator, including his last position as executive vice president. Fr. Leahy holds a Ph.D. in history from Stanford University, an M.A. in U.S. history from Saint Louis University, and master's degrees in divinity and sacred theology from the Jesuit School of Theology in Berkeley, California. He is the author of *Adapting to America: Catholics, Jesuits and Higher Education in the Twentieth Century* as well as scholarly articles on religious and educational history in the United States. Fr. Leahy is a trustee of Santa Clara and Creighton universities.

ROBERT R. NEWTON is special assistant to the president of Boston College. He holds a B.A. (summa cum laude) from the University of Scranton, and graduate degrees from Woodstock College (Ph.L., S.T.B.), Yale University (S.T.M.), and Harvard University (Ed.M., Ed.D). He served as headmaster of Regis High School in New York City and was on the faculty of the University of San Francisco before coming to Boston College as associate academic vice president in 1980. During his 35-year tenure at Boston College, he has been involved in university-wide academic planning, assessment, and accreditation issues. He has published a variety of articles on models of curriculum and academic organization topics.

DAVID J. O'BRIEN, an early contributor to the field of American Catholic studies, received his B.A. from the University of Notre Dame and his Ph.D. from the University of Rochester, and completed postdoctoral study at Harvard Divinity School. He is professor emeritus at the College of the Holy Cross where he was the Loyola Professor of Roman Catholic Studies. Most recently he held the University Professorship of Faith and Culture at the University of Dayton. O'Brien served as president of the American Catholic Historical Association. He is widely published in the field of American Catholic history and his more popular writings can be found inside the pages of such publications as *America* magazine. Long concerned with the relationship between civic and religious life, O'Brien has been a social activist since his early involvement in the Vietnam War protests.